Songs and Activities for Best, Best Friends

A Complete Music Curriculum for Early Childhood

"Guitar Bob" Messano

Songs Notated by John Sheehan

THE CENTER FOR APPLIED
RESEARCH IN EDUCATION
West Nyack, New York 10995

Dedication

in living memory of my father, Frank P. Messano

With Appreciation

to my mother, Marilyn,
for filling our home with art and love;
to my wife, Betsy,
for always being beside me;
to my friend, John Sheehan,
for taking me fishing in the middle of a song;
to the preschool directors and teachers,
for their love of children;
to the children,
for teaching me.

Library of Congress Cataloging-in-Publication Data

Messano, Bob, 1958-
    Songs and activities for best, best friends : a complete music curriculum for early childhood / "Guitar Bob" Messano ; songs notated by John Sheehan.
                    p. cm.
            ISBN 0-87628-796-8
    1. Singing—Instruction and study—Juvenile. 2. School music—
    Instruction and study. I. Sheehan, John. II. Title.
            MT898.M47 1991
372.87′043—dc20   90-2001
                                                       CIP
                                                        MN

ISBN 0-87628-796-8

**THE CENTER FOR APPLIED
RESEARCH IN EDUCATION
BUSINESS & PROFESSIONAL DIVISION**
A division of Simon & Schuster
West Nyack, New York 10995

Printed in the United States of America

About the Author

Bob Messano, better known as "Guitar Bob," is a composer and performer of original children's songs. He presently works as an early childhood music specialist at more than twenty pre-schools in New Jersey. Children enthusiastically respond to his friendly and imaginative style of sharing songs. As a result, educators and parents have commended his musical programs.

"Guitar Bob" earned his B.A. in Early Childhood Education from William Paterson College in Wayne, N.J. As an undergraduate, he composed songs for two- , three- , and four-year-old children included in a *Preschool Curriculum Activities Library* by Anthony and Kathleen Coletta (published by the Center for Applied Research in Education in 1986). Many teachers have benefited from using these materials and by participating in his workshops and musical development courses at the college level.

Over the past five years, "Guitar Bob" has entertained, educated and involved his audiences. His concerts feature an exciting blend of acoustic guitar and harmonica playing, singalongs, and opportunities for creative expression through movement. He has performed at preschools, elementary schools, special education facilities, camps, libraries, folk festivals and environmental centers. In the future, he plans to continue recording his songs; publishing materials for teachers, children and their families; and giving musical performances and workshops across the country.

FOR BOOKING INFORMATION:

Guitar Bob
P.O. Box 470
Oak Ridge, NJ 07438

About the Song Notator

John Sheehan is a talented all-around musician who has mastered several instruments. He is a composer, teacher, and performer who has combined the influences of classical music training with a modern sensibility to create an improvisational style all his own. His colorful instrumentation and voice can be heard on the tape which accompanies this book.

Introduction

Welcome to *Songs and Activities for Best, Best Friends*! The purpose of the songs, activities, and pictures in this book and the accompanying tape is to create an atmosphere of friendly musical exchange among early childhood teachers, children, and parents (Music-Grams are a nice way to bring parents into the circle of song; see pp. vi–vii). As music flows from one person to another, we become participants in a form of communication integrally related to the past, present, and future of human development. Songs serve a myriad of functions. They transmit history and culture, provide an outlet for our emotions and creativity, and serve as a common ground to enjoy life with others.

The organization of this book proceeds along lines of feelings as well as concrete curriculum areas. For example, Section One, "A Sense of Belonging," presents songs which support the child's self-esteem along with activities that reinforce the child's pride through *art*. Section Two, "A Sense of Humor," uses funny songs as a vehicle of *language arts* development. Section Three, "A Sense of Wonder," opens doors of *science* through imaginative songs. Section Four, "A Sense of Friendship," is comprised of songs which encourage kindness towards others and is thus a natural bridge to *social studies*.

Within each section you will find all of the resources—the songs, activities and illustrations—you need to transmit the music and its message to children. You are the essential human element in making the songs meaningful for them! Although it is not as important to be able to read music as it is to communicate a sincere love of music to children, you may find that some of the following suggestions can help you discover the song melodies:

- Seek out a musician-friend to work *with* you in translating the written symbols into songs. Taking part in the process will enable you to gradually build some music-reading skills in a supportive environment. Tape-record the melodies for future reference.

- Learn to play the chords of the songs (written above the music staff) on an instrument. An autoharp (electric autoharps sound great and don't go out of tune), nylon-string guitar, or ukelele are relatively easy for beginners to play. Sing along to the chord-changes in a natural, conversational voice. You'll probably come very close to the written melody in this way.

- Use a computer to help you read the music! Music software is available which enables you to place the notes on the staff and to play them back.

- Learn to read music through a course of study and/or instrument lessons. It's much more practical and fun to learn music theory while you're learning to play an instrument. As with young children, learning through hands-on experiences seems to be the most rewarding approach in the long run.

- Create your own melodies to go along with the words! If you are confident and creative you can make this method work. Children are very appreciative of music in a broad sense; they will enjoy the individuality of your voice and be inspired by it when they are creating their own music.

- Use the accompanying audiocassette to get a feel for the styles of music explored in the book and to learn the ten songs provided.

The songs in this book were created in the playful spirit of early childhood. Children ages two through six will be able to appreciate and respond to the songs in ways that parallel their development. For example, a three-year-old may enjoy making a sheep sound in the song "She-Bop" (see pg. 95), while a five-year-old will perform a variety of characterizations based on the same lyrics. A sensitive teacher can also simplify, repeat, or adapt songs in ways that her particular group of children enjoys most.

The activities presented in partnership with each song are also designed with real classroom situations in mind. Each plan consists of three parts: "Awakening" introduces the song to children through stimulating words, materials, and experiences; "Celebrating" gives the children the freedom to creatively interpret the lyrics through singing, playing games, moving their bodies, exploring instruments, dramatizing, using puppets and props, etc.; "Embracing" provides opportunities for the children to extend their learning through related activities in art, language arts, science, and social studies.

The advantage of this three-part plan is that it can be used in sections at the teacher's discretion. Variations and adaptations are expected and encouraged as you enhance these activities with your own individuality, creativity, and teaching style. Always consider whether the given activity is appropriate for the skills of the age group you are working with. If it isn't, use the activity's ideas as the raw material for a simpler or more elaborate plan.

In closing, I would like to explain how I came to select the title, *Songs and Activities for Best, Best Friends*, and the activity plan terms—Awakening, Celebrating, and Embracing. I hope this explanation, based on real-life experiences, will give you further insight into the beautiful world of children's music.

One day, while waiting for my wife outside of her kindergarten class, I overheard one child say to another in a voice filled with the promise of some great bargain, "I'll be your best, best friend in the whole wide world!" I was struck with the realization that friendship is like a crown jewel of the early childhood years, representing the complex ability to successfully deal with others from a position of self-assuredness.

The terms of the activity-plan represent a philosophy of "what early childhood should be" that has unfolded like the wings of a songbird through all of my joyful experiences with children and teachers alike. The following anecdotes are but a few of the many magical encounters I have been priviledged to be a part of:

Awakening . . .

I am playing my guitar and singing at an infant center. The oldest children there are only two-year-olds. They're sitting in the front row in small plastic chairs. Babies in high chairs are the proverbial "peanut gallery" behind them. While the older children are singing a song about animals, a baby joins in. The teacher and I look at each other in astonishment. She brings the baby to the front row seats!

Celebrating . . .

A nursery school is celebrating "Father–Child Day" at a mountain park. John Sheehan, who notated the songs in this book, is picking his mandolin while I strum the guitar and sing "We'll Be the House" (see pg. 51). The young children spontaneously create their own circle game, skipping beneath the outstretched arms of two older children who pretend to be the "house." This wonderful wheel spins as the fathers look on with smiles.

Embracing . . .

A grassy summer hillside is dotted with children, chanting along to "The Tree's Song" (see pg. 149) and keeping the rhythm on their bodies. At the end of the song, many children give me gifts of grass roots freshly pulled in response to the line, "We've all got roots in the ground!"

    I hope these songs and activities will contribute to a world of friendship between children and in turn between all people. Use them with joy!

Guitar Bob

Music-Gram

(sample note to parents)

Dear Parents,

In the spirit of getting to know one another, the children learned a new song. It's called "I Like You Very Much." Here are the lyrics:

> I like you very much!
> I like you very much!
> I like to whisper in your ear . . .
> I like you very much!
>
> I want to be your friend!
> I want to be your friend!
> I like to whisper in your ear . . .
> I want to be your friend!
>
> I want to play with you!
> I want to play with you!
> I like to whisper in your ear . . .
> I want to play with you!

(repeat first verse)

This song helps children learn to touch one another in friendly, non-threatening ways. Our class often winds up in giggles and hugs after singing it. Ask your child to share the tune with you and you can enjoy it too!

Do you share gentle times with your child? In our fast-paced world we may sometimes forget the importance of a quiet, soothing voice; a special moment of observing the world around us; or a praising word, gesture, or gift. Taking the few minutes to *learn this song with your child* is a great way to slow down the world to a friendly speed.

Try singing this singing this song with your child every day for a week. Change the lyrics, if you like, responding to different life-situations that come up. For example, if your child gives you a flower you can sing . . .

> I thank you very much!
> I thank you very much!
> I like to whisper in your ear . . .
> I thank you very much!

Let me know how the song works at home!

Music-Gram

(sample note to parents)

Dear Parents,

Following our wonderful visit to the zoo, the children learned a new song. It's called "Will You Be My Cuddly Panda Bear?" Here are the lyrics:

Will you be my cuddly panda bear?
Will you be my cuddly panda bear?
If you'll be my panda bear, I will be your polar bear . . .
Will you be my cuddly panda bear?

Will you be my fuzzy caterpillar?
Will you be my fuzzy caterpillar?
If you'll be my caterpillar, I will be your big 'gorillar' . . .
Will you be my fuzzy caterpillar?

Will you be my lovely little mouse?
Will you be my lovely little mouse?
If you'll be my little mouse, I will be your speckled grouse . . .
Will you be my lovely little mouse?

Will you be my sweet and shaggy moose?
Will you be my sweet and shaggy moose?
If you'll be my shaggy moose, I will be your silly goose . . .
Will you be my sweet and shaggy moose?

As you can plainly see, you can make all kinds of silly additions to this song with your child. However, you don't necessarily need to sing the whole song to have fun. For example, sing the first line and see what kind of response your child will come up with. An exchange of creative, silly ideas may ensue, such as the following:

Parent: Will you be my cuddly panda bear?
Child: Yes, I'll be your bear!
Parent: Would you like some very yummy honey?
Child: Yes, I'd like to put it in my tummy!

If you'd like help learning the tune of the song, I'll be glad to share it with you! See you soon!

Contents

2 A SENSE OF HUMOR, 53

This section integrates music and language arts.

3 A SENSE OF WONDER, 105

This section integrates music and science.

4 A SENSE OF FRIENDSHIP, 157

This section integrates music and social studies.

APPENDIX, 209

Reproducible patterns and charts for music activities.

Section 1

A Sense of Belonging (Music-art activities)

This section integrates music and art. The songs and activities are particularly suitable for building children's confidence in themselves and their social environment. Children are encouraged to grow in feelings of self-worth and accomplishment.

Camp Sleepy	*tipi mural*
Everybody's Smilin' at the Pet Store	*cookie cutters with playdough*
Giant Steps	*feet painting*
How Old Are You?	*birthday collages*
I Can Make a Little Sound!	*playdough*
I'm Holdin' Teacher's Hand Today	*handprint mural*
I'm on My Way to School	*exploring puzzles*
I'm So Strong	*sportspeoples' collage*
I Know a Little Bug	*cardboard "Hug Bug"*
In My Home	*making finger puppets*
It's Nice to Say Hello	*paperbag puppets*
A Little Birdy Told Me	*popsicle-stick birds*
Looky, Looky, Looky	*crayon "Discovery Book"*
The Measuring Song	*body posters*
My Favorite Colors	*color-mixing experiments*
Nobody Else Is Quite Like Me	*paper plate "Veg-a-Buddy"*
Our Train	*group mural*
Pick Me Up in an Airplane	*imaginary vehicles*
Sittin' in a Circle!	*fingerpainting*
Sometimes I Feel Happy!	*masks*
Telephone Call	*tactile phone numbers*
That Hat	*paper plate sombreros*
Toys on the Shelf	*"Book of Favorite Toys"*
Up in My Treehouse	*tempera painting*
We'll Be the House	*making a playhouse*

1

Title: Camp Sleepy

Skills: reads symbols
discusses feelings and fears
helps create a mural

Development: **Materials:**

A. Awakening . . .

Make a rebus chart with the words to the song, substituting   oak tag
simple sketches for the following words: *teepee, sticks, fire, pan,*   markers
bear, tree (see Appendix, pg. 210). Invite the children to read
along with you as you point to the words and symbols.
Display the rebus chart in the "Library/Language Area" of
the classroom for the children to read independently.

B. Celebrating . . .

Provide baby dolls for the children to rock to sleep while you sing   baby dolls
this lullaby. Model the action by wrapping one of the dolls in a   blankets
blanket and rocking along with them.
Discuss things that can be frightening at night (strange
sounds, monsters, the bear in the song, bad dreams, etc.). Reas-
sure the children that most scary things in the night are not real
and their parents are there to keep them safe.

C. Embracing . . .

Let the children create a teepee mural! Pin up a large sheet of   butcher paper
butcher paper on which you have drawn a teepee outline. Provide   pushpins
tempera paint and paintbrushes for the children to use in creat-   tempera paint
ing their own Native American symbols and designs.   paintbrushes
Display the teepee on the wall of the classroom. Invite par-
ents to a Native American celebration where the children perform the song, share special foods, dance, etc.

(lullaby)

words and music:
Bob Messano

Camp Sleepy

Great Bear walks in the night-time! Drums on a hol-low tree---! But,

I'll be safe, in-side my sack, if he comes look-in' for me---!

CHORUS:

Come in-to Camp Slee-py! Crawl in-to my tee-pee! Who is up, to

bring the sticks, to start the morn-in' fire? It's clink-a-clink as

ma-ma gets the pan, to put the corn-meal in! But, I'm way down in my

sleep-in' sack... Back in ol' Dream-land! Come in-to Camp

Slee-py! Crawl in-to my tee-pee! Who is up, to

bring the sticks, to start the morn-in' fire?

2. Snow Owl lives in a white tree!
   Hoots like a cryin' baby!
   Tiny Mouse is at my door . . .
   Won't somebody hide me?

   (CHORUS)

3. Grey Wolf sings on the mountain!
   Must be feelin' lonely!
   Pull my covers over me . . .
   Shut my eyes so tightly!

3

Title: Everybody's Smilin' at the Pet Store

Skills: plays imaginatively
expresses choice; performs pantomime
manipulates playdough

Development: **Materials:**

A. Awakening . . .

Create a "Pretend Pet Store" in the classroom. Provide props,   pet store props
such as: stuffed animals, cardboard boxes with windows cut out
(representing cages or aquariums), a real birdcage, a play cash
register with play money, empty boxes of pet food, etc.
　　Encourage the children to work, play, and shop in the store.
Talk to the children about their own pets or pets they would like
to have.

B. Celebrating . . .

Invite the children to bring their favorite stuffed animals to a   stuffed animals
singalong. Sing the song and ask each child in turn to name their
favorite kind of pet.
　　For variation, encourage each child to pantomime their favorite pets while the other children try to guess its identity.

C. Embracing . . .

Let the children explore animal shapes using cookie cutters and   cookie cutters
playdough! Provide cookie cutters in familiar shapes such as bird,   playdough
cat, dog, duck, fish, and rabbit. Encourage the children to form a
variety of animal shapes.
　　Extend the children's thinking by asking what their animals like to eat, like to do, where they live, etc.

FREE
Goldfish
Today!

4

(cheerfully)

words and music:
Bob Messano

Everybody's Smilin' at the Pet Store

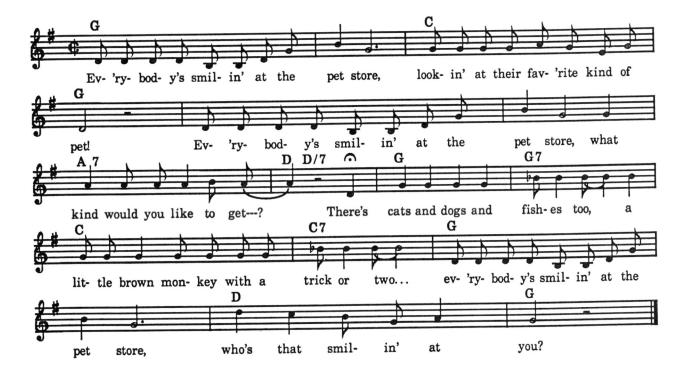

Ev-'ry-bod-y's smil-in' at the pet store, look-in' at their fav-'rite kind of pet! Ev-'ry-bod-y's smil-in' at the pet store, what kind would you like to get---? There's cats and dogs and fish-es too, a lit-tle brown mon-key with a trick or two... ev-'ry-bod-y's smil-in' at the pet store, who's that smil-in' at you?

Variation:

(Child's name)'s smilin' at the pet store,
Lookin' for his/her fav'rite kind of pet!
(Child's name)'s smilin' at the pet store,
What kind would you like to get?

There's cat's and dogs and fishes, too,
A little brown monkey with a trick or two . . .
(Child's name)'s smilin' at the pet store,
Who's that smilin' at you?

5

Title: **Giant Steps**

Skills: follows directions in a game
performs a variety of walks to music
paints with feet

Development: **Materials:**

A. Awakening . . .

Take the class for a walk in the neighborhood park or play-yard.   none
Pick a nearby object (tree, rock, slide, etc.) and challenge the
children to take little, big or giant steps to get there.
    Give the children the opportunity to lead the game by choos-
ing new objects and new kinds of steps (for example: a silly step, a
dinosaur step, a bouncy step, a baby step, etc.).

B. Celebrating . . .

Stick pre-cut, colored self-stick vinyl footprints on the floor of the   footprint
classroom (see Appendix, pg. 211). Sing the song while walking   pattern
along the footprints. Encourage the children to follow your exam-   self-stick vinyl
ple. Praise their efforts!   scissors
    Make a tape recording of the song and teach the children to   tape recorder
use the tape recorder independently. Encourage them to rein-   cassette tape
terpret the song.
    Use the footprints for other walking and marching songs
over time.

C. Embracing . . .

Let the children paint with their feet! Spread a large sheet of   butcher paper
butcher paper across the floor. Provide plastic plates filled with   plastic plates
various colors of tempera paint.   tempera paint
    Guide the children in removing shoes and socks, dipping   washbasin
their bare feet in paint, walking across the paper, and washing   soapy water
up.   paper towels

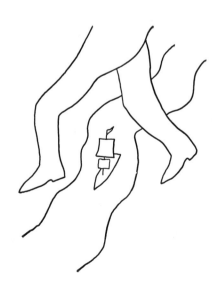

words and music:
Bob Messano

Giant Steps

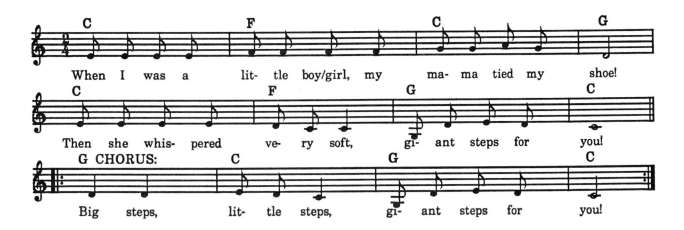

When I was a lit- tle boy/girl, my ma- ma tied my shoe!

Then she whis- pered ve- ry soft, gi- ant steps for you!

CHORUS: Big steps, lit- tle steps, gi- ant steps for you!

2. Babies take their baby steps,
In their baby shoes!
'Til somebody says to them,
Giant steps for you!

(CHORUS)

3. Go and take a little step,
Take a big one, too!
Pretty soon it's giant steps,
Giant steps for you!

(CHORUS)

4. Walkin' over bridges,
The water looks so blue!
Callin' out to all my friends,
Giant steps for you!

(CHORUS)

Title: **How Old Are You?**

Skills: responds to poetry
socializes/dances with other children
creates a collage

Development: **Materials:**

A. Awakening . . .

Share the following poem: words to poem

> A Birthday Tree is growing,
> For every girl and boy,
> And all the buds are wishes,
> And all the leaves are toys!
>
> And high up in the branches,
> Where no one else can see,
> We'll have a Birthday Party,
> And sip our lemon tea!

Ask each child to share a birthday wish.

B. Celebrating . . .

Sing the song to a child who is having a birthday.   party hats
    Invite all of the children to a "Birthday Dance." Encourage   record player
them to wear party hats while they dance to favorite records.   records

C. Embracing . . .

Let the children create birthday collages! Provide bits of wrap-   wrapping paper
ping paper, ribbon and bows to be cut and pasted onto construc-   construction
tion paper. Encourage the children to talk about what they like   paper
most about birthdays.   ribbon
    Display the collages on a bulletin board or wall decorated   bows
like a "Birthday Tree."   paste
                                   scissors

(gently)

words and music:
Bob Messano

How Old Are You?

How old are you? Hold your fing- ers up! Are you old- er than a kit- ten? Or young- er than a pup? How old are you? Whis- per it to me! To- ge- ther we'll go danc- ing a- round the birth- day tree!

2. When a little boy/girl turns one,
   He/She has alot of fun!
   When a little boy/girl turns two,
   There's alot that he/she can do!
   When a little boy/girl turns three,
   He's/She's clever as can be . . .
   Together we'll go dancing around the birthday tree!

3. Four and five and six,
   Pass you very quick!
   Seven, eight and nine,
   Slip away in time!
   Growin' like a wave that sparkles on the sea . . .
   Together we'll go dancin' around the birthday tree!

   (repeat first verse)

Title: **I Can Make a Little Sound**

Skills: explores a xylophone

plays an instrument; dances to music

adapts song lyrics to other activities

Development:	Materials:

A. Awakening . . .

Make xylophones available for the children to explore. Develop a system so that every child who wants a turn to play can do so in a reasonable amount of time.

Play a game by asking the children to match the sounds you make on a xylophone. For example, play a note softly, play it loudly, play a bunch of notes in ascending/descending order. Let the children take turns being the music-maker while others match their sounds.

xylophones

B. Celebrating . . .

Ask the children to play instruments while you sing the song. In addition to xylophones; invite them to explore the following: jingle bells, finger cymbals, triangles, etc.

For variation, ask some of the children to pretend that they are wind-up music box dancers while the others play. The dancers can hold or wear flowing scarves as they move. Challenge them to wind themselves down at the end of the song.

instruments
scarves

C. Embracing . . .

Let the children adapt the song while molding playdough! For example, sing or chant the following while rolling the playdough on the table:

playdough

I can make a squiggle snake!
Hiss! Hiss! Hiss!
I can make a squiggle snake!
Hiss! Hiss! Hiss!

Hiss! Hiss! Hiss!
I give my friends a kiss!
I can make a squiggle snake!
Hiss! Hiss! Hiss!

words and music:
Bob Messano

I Can Make a Little Sound

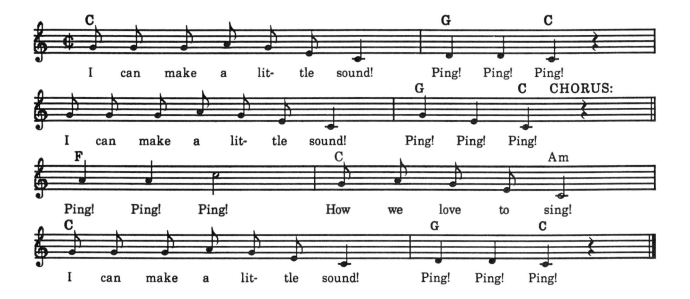

I can make a lit- tle sound! Ping! Ping! Ping!

I can make a lit- tle sound! Ping! Ping! Ping! CHORUS:

Ping! Ping! Ping! How we love to sing!

I can make a lit- tle sound! Ping! Ping! Ping!

2. I can hear a drop of rain!
Ping! Ping! Ping!
I can hear a drop of rain!
Ping! Ping! Ping!

(CHORUS)

3. I can hear the music box!
Ping! Ping! Ping!
I can hear the music box!
Ping! Ping! Ping!

(CHORUS)

4. I can hear a little bell!
Ping! Ping! Ping!
I can hear a little bell!
Ping, Ping, Ping!

(CHORUS)

11

Title: **I'm Holdin' Teacher's Hand Today**

Skills: responds to poetry
plays a cooperative game
paints with hands

Development: **Materials:**

A. Awakening . . .

Share the following poem: words to poem

> *There was a boy named Billy,*
> *Who came to school one day.*
> *He couldn't find his mommy,*
> *And he couldn't find his way.*
>
> *The teacher saw him crying,*
> *And whispered in his ear,*
> *We'll have fun together,*
> *And mom will soon be here!*

Ask the children why Billy felt sad. How did the teacher help
him?

B. Celebrating . . .

Play a cooperative game, as follows: dress-up clothes
Divide the children into two groups: teachers and children.
You can differentiate the groups by having the teachers wear
scarves and the children wear hats, etc. Help everyone choose a
partner from the other group.
Encourage the children to skip around the room to the music
while holding hands. Trade places and repeat.

C. Embracing . . .

Let the children make a handprint mural. Label a large sheet of   butcher block
butcher paper with the words, "Hands Are for Holding!" Provide   paper
plastic plates filled with various colors of tempera paint and   plastic plates
encourage the children to dip their hands into the paint.   tempera paint
While the children make handprints on the paper, ask them   marker
what else hands can be used for. Write down their names and
ideas next to their handprints.

**words and music:
Bob Messano**

(warmly)

I'm Holdin' Teacher's Hand Today

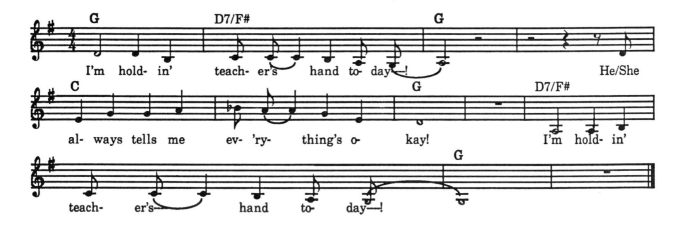

I'm hold- in' teach- er's hand to day—! He/She

al- ways tells me ev- 'ry- thing's o- kay! I'm hold- in'

teach- er's—— hand to day——!

2. I will walk by teacher's side today!
   See what kind of games he/she likes to play!
   I will walk by teacher's side today!

3. I will dance a happy dance today!
   Love to hear my teacher's tuba play!
   I will dance a happy dance today!

(repeat first verse)

Title: **I'm on My Way to School**

Skills: relates personal experiences
performs motions to a song
explores puzzles

Development: **Materials:**

A. Awakening . . .

Bring in a box filled with the following common household ob-   box
jects: bar of soap, towel, toothbrush, toothpaste, cereal box, bowl,   household
spoon, cup, etc.   objects
    Reach into the box and pull out the objects one at a time.
Ask the children to raise their hand if they used that object in the
morning.
    Place some of the objects, such as the cereal box and bowl, in
the "Family Area" for the children to handle and play with.

B. Celebrating . . .

Sing the song and perform the motions suggested by the lyrics.   none
Add verses to the song based on experiences that the children
suggest. For example:

> *I get up in the morning and I make my lunch . . .*
> *I get up in the morning and I tie my shoes . . .*
> *I get up in the morning and I drink my milk . . .*
> *I get up in the morning and I jog to school.*

C. Embracing . . .

Let the children explore puzzles made from the front side of cereal   cereal boxes
boxes. To make the puzzles, cut out the front side of the cereal box   scissors
and cover it on both sides with clear self-stick vinyl. Cut the   self-stick vinyl
puzzle into three or more pieces, according to the children's age
and skill.
    As the children figure out the puzzles, ask them to name
their favorite kinds of cereal, as well as other breakfast foods that
they enjoy.

(sprightly)

words and music:
Bob Messano

I'm on My Way to School

I get up in the morn- ing and I wash my face, I wash my face, I wash my face! I get up in the morn- ing and I wash my face, and I'm on my way to school!

2. I get up in the morning and I comb my hair,
   I comb my hair, I comb my hair!
   I get up in the morning and I comb my hair,
   And I'm on my way to school!

3. I get up in the morning and I brush my teeth,
   I brush my teeth, I brush my teeth!
   I get up in the morning and I brush my teeth,
   And I'm on my way to school!

4. I go with my mommy/daddy in a great big car,
   A great big car, A great big car!
   I go with my mommy/daddy in a great big car,
   And I'm on my way to school!

Title: **I'm So Strong**

Skills: exercises large muscles
performs body movements to music
creates a collage

Development: **Materials:**

A. Awakening . . .

Bring in a small hand-held barbell with light weights. Give each   barbell
child a turn trying to lift the barbell, as you guide them for safety.
Praise each child's efforts!
    Visit a local gymnasium or fitness center! Ask an instructor
to demonstrate weightlifting for the children.

B. Celebrating . . .

Encourage the children to act out the song by showing off their   rhythm
muscles and pretending to lift weights.   instruments
    Give half of the children rhythm instruments (tone blocks,
tamborines, rhythm sticks, etc.) to play while the others do a
workout to the beat. Trade places and repeat.

C. Embracing . . .

Let the children make a collage of muscular athletes-in-action!   newspapers
Provide newspaper and magazine photos of athletes performing   sports
vigorously. Encourage the children to cut out the pictures (pre-   magazines
cut the pictures for younger children) and paste them on large   scissors
sheets of construction paper.
    Teach the children the names of different muscles.   paste
                                                                       construction
                                                                          paper

words and music:
Bob Messano

I'm So Strong

I'm so strong! I'm so strong! Look how strong I— am!

2. Muscles here! Muscles there!
Look how strong I am!
Muscles here! Muscles there!
Look how strong I am!

(CHORUS)

3. Liftin' weights! I feel great!
Look how strong I am!
Liftin' weights! I feel great!
Look how strong I am!

(CHORUS)

Title: **I Know a Little Bug**

Skills: investigates new materials
plays a cooperative game
shows affection to others

Development: **Materials:**

  A. Awakening . . .

Twist colorful pipecleaners into various bug shapes (spider, cater-   pipe cleaners
pillar, bee, ant, butterfly, etc.). Place them in the "Science/
Discovery Area" of the classroom for the children to touch and
investigate.
Encourage the children to count and compare the number of
legs, wings, antennae, etc. Ask the children which bugs they
think look friendly and which look not-so-friendly.

  B. Celebrating . . .

Invite the children to play a cooperative musical game, as follows: none
Sing the song and choose a child to come up and get a hug.
Ask each child what kind of bug they are. Respond with a simple
direction, depending on what kind of bug they are. For example:

Fly home, butterfly!

Buzz away, bee!

Crawl back, caterpillar!

  C. Embracing . . .

Let the children help make a "Hug Bug" to hang in the classroom!   cardboard
Provide a large cardboard cut-out in the shape of a ladybug. Give   scissors
the children pre-cut circles made from black construction paper.   construction
Ask them to paste the spots on the ladybug's back.   paper
Punch a hole in the completed ladybug and suspend it from   paste
the ceiling with string. Whenever someone stands under it, give   hole puncher
them a hug. Praise the children as they follow your example and   string
begin their own hugging games.

(affectionately)

words and music:
Bob Messano

I Know a Little Bug

I know a lit- tle bug! I wan- na give a hug! And
that lit- tle bug is you!

Title: In My Home

Skills: names family members
claps to music; plays a cooperative game
creates finger puppets

Development: **Materials:**

A. Awakening . . .

Share a family photo album with the children. Talk about things   photo album
that you liked to do when you were a child. Name the members of
your immediate family and show their pictures.
Ask each child in turn to name the members of his/her
family.

B. Celebrating . . .

Play a cooperative musical game, as follows: none
Ask the children to stand in a circle. Choose two children to
stand in the center. Sing the song in a lively manner while
clapping the beat. Ask the children in the center to choose two
more people to be in their family (to join them in the center).
Continue until everyone has been chosen!

C. Embracing . . .

Let the children make a whole family of finger puppets! Provide   puppet patterns
them with several pre-cut paper puppet shapes (see Appendix,   scissors
page 212). Encourage them to use crayons or colored pencils to   crayons/colored
draw in the features, hair, and clothes on their puppets.   pencils
Tape the puppets to fit on the children's fingers. Have a   tape
"Family Puppet Show" where the children can introduce their
puppets by name and show what they can do.

words and music:
Bob Messano

In My Home

(unaccompanied)

Fine

In my home! In my home! I've got a fam- 'ly, in my home!

D.C. al Fine

O- pen up your arms and let your fam- 'ly in!

2. In my home! In my home!
I've got a mother/father in my home!
In my home! In my home!
I've got a mother/father in my home!

Open up your arms and let your mother/father in!
Open up your arms and let your mother/father in!

3. In my home! In my home!
I've got a brother/sister in my home!
In my home! In my home!
I've got a brother/sister in my home!

Open up your arms and let your brother/sister in!
Open up your arms and let your brother/sister in!

(repeat first verse)

Title: **It's Nice to Say Hello**

Skills: responds to puppetry
adapts songs
creates a puppet

Development:

Materials:

Development: **Materials:**

A. Awakening . . .

Introduce the children to a paper lunch bag puppet. Have the puppet greet each child individually.
    Demonstrate the song using the puppet. After the children become familiar with the lyrics, have the puppet change the word "toes" for humorous effect. For example:

You can say it with a wiggle of your (ears)!

lunch bag
markers

B. Celebrating . . .

Encourage the children to perform the motions and expressions suggested by the lyrics. Let them take turns leading the song
Use the song to greet classroom visitors, including parents.
Adapt the song for the end of the day, as follows:

Bye-Bye! Bye-Bye!
It's time to say bye-bye . . .

C Embracing . . .

Let the children make a friendly lunch bag puppet! Provide paper lunch bags, scissors, glue, buttons, cotton balls, and a variety of other art materials which you have on hand. Encourage the children to create individual features on their puppets.
    Invite all the children and their puppets to a singalong. Sing favorite songs!

lunch bags
scissors
glue
buttons
cotton balls
assorted art
   materials

(cheerfully)

words and music:
Bob Messano

It's Nice to Say Hello

Hel- lo   Hel- lo!   It's   nice to say hel-   lo!   lo!   You can

say it with a wave! You can   say it with a smile! You can   say it with a wig- gle of your

toe! Hel-   lo!   Hel-   lo!   It's   nice   to   say   hel-   lo!

23

Title: **A Little Birdy Told Me**

Skills: shows curiosity

expresses "likes"; performs creative movements

creates a puppet

Development: **Materials:**

A. Awakening . . .

Place some feathers inside a "Feely Box" (this is a box whose
contents can be felt, but not seen). Encourage the children to try
and guess what is inside by reaching in and touching.

When all the children have had a chance to guess, open the
box and show them what was inside. Pass the feathers around for
the children to look at. Reply to their questions and observations.

"Feely Box"

feathers

B. Celebrating . . .

Sing the song as a transition to "Play Time." Ask each child to
name and/or describe something that he/she would like to do in
the classroom.

Challenge the children to "fly like birds" over to the places
where they would like to play.

C. Embracing . . .

Let the children make their own "Feathered Friends" stick puppets! Provide puppet patterns for the children to choose from (see
Appendix, pg. 213), as well as crayons and colorful feathers for
decoration. Guide them in gluing on wooden craft sticks for handles (representing bird feet).

Share in the spirit of talking to the children's creations. Ask
the children to show you how the birds fly, hop, dig for worms, etc.

puppet patterns

crayons

feathers

wooden craft
  sticks

glue

words and music:
Bob Messano

A Little Birdy Told Me

A lit- tle bird- y told me, some- thin' 'bout you!

Told me all the things, that you like to do! Can you tell me, lit- tle

bird- y, all the things that you like to do?

Variations:

A little froggy . . .

A little bunny . . .

A little puppy . . .

etc.

Title: **Looky, Looky, Looky**

Skills: explores the environment
shows imaginative thinking
describes artwork

Development: **Materials:**

A. Awakening . . .

Take the children on a "Discovery Walk." Give each child a paper   lunch bags
lunch bag for collecting interesting finds. Encourage the children
to explore a natural area (park, patch of grass, area beneath a
tree, etc.).

Locate yourself on a blanket or bench where the children
can come to share their discoveries. Challenge the children to find
someone else who has a match to one of their objects.

B. Celebrating . . .

Play an imaginative thinking game as follows: none
Sing the song and ask the children to pretend they have
found something. Ask them to tell everyone what it is.

Extend the game by choosing a category (things that are
found in the park, at the zoo, in a house, etc.) and challenging the
children to name something that belongs in it.

C. Embracing . . .

Let the children make a class "Discovery Book." Provide them   white paper
with crayons and paper and encourage them to make a picture of   crayons
some they have found or pretended to find.   stapler
Label the pictures with the children's comments. Staple the
book together and place it in the "Library/Language Area" of the
classroom for the children to look through independently.

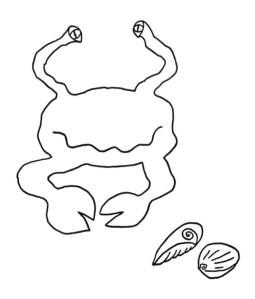

26

(jubilantly)

words and music:
Bob Messano

Looky, Looky, Looky

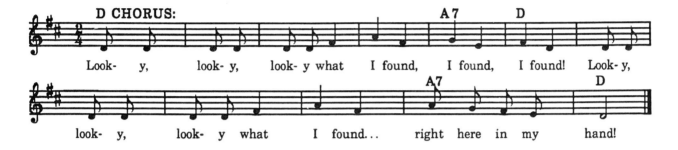

Look- y, look- y, look- y what I found, I found, I found! Look- y,
look- y, look- y what I found... right here in my hand!

1. I found a little bit of sunshine!
   Sunshine! Sunshine!
   I found a little bit of sunshine . . .
   Right here in my hand!

   (CHORUS)

2. I found a beautiful flower!
   A flower! A flower!
   I found a beautiful flower . . .
   Right here in my hand!

   (CHORUS)

3. I found a little green froggy!
   A froggy! A froggy!
   I found a little green froggy . . .
   Right here in my hand!

   (CHORUS)

4. I found a colorful rainbow!
   A rainbow! A rainbow!
   I found a colorful rainbow . . .
   Right here in my hand!

   (CHORUS)

Title: **The Measuring Song**

Skills: responds to poetry
uses a prop to enliven a song
completes a large-scale artwork

Development:

Materials:

A. Awakening . . .

Share the following poem with the children:

words to poem

> When I was small,
> I used to crawl,
> I spent the whole day crawling.
> But when I tried to stand up tall . . .
> I spent the whole day falling!

Ask the children to think of things that they can do now that they couldn't do as babies.

B. Celebrating . . .

Measure each child with a length of yarn. Cut the yarn equal to the child's height and let them hold it.

ball of yarn
scissors

Encourage the children to interpret the song by measuring themselves and their friends with the yarn.

Let the children take home their piece of yarn for further creative uses!

C. Embracing . . .

Let the children make full-sized body posters! Spread large sheets of butcher paper on the floor and ask the children to lie down on them. Trace the outline of their bodies with a marker. Provide colorful markers for the children to draw in their features and clothes.

butcher paper
markers
glue
yarn

Encourage the children to enhance their posters by gluing on pieces of yarn for hair.

words and music:
Bob Messano

The Measuring Song

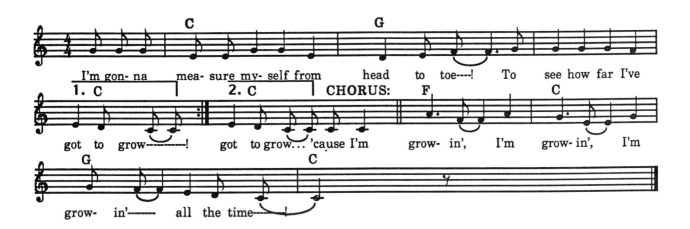

I'm gon- na mea- sure my- self from head to toe----! To see how far I've

1. C — got to grow----------! 2. C — got to grow... 'cause I'm CHORUS: F grow- in', I'm C grow- in', I'm

G grow- in'------ all the time------

2. I'm gonna measure myself from knee to knee . . .
To see how wide that I might be!

(repeat)

(CHORUS)

3. I'm gonna measure myself from hand to hand . . .
Stretch myself across the land!

(repeat)

(CHORUS)

4. I'm gonna measure myself from ear to ear . . .
There's a whole lotta brains that I keep in here!

(repeat)

(CHORUS)

5. I'm gonna measure my friends from head to toe . . .
To see how far they've got to grow!

(repeat)

(CHORUS)

Title: My Favorite Colors

Skills: plays a cooperative game
expresses "likes"
experiments with color combinations

Development: **Materials:**

A. Awakening . . .

Invite the children to play a cooperative game, as follows: none
Ask the children to think of colors that they would like to be.
Approach one child and say,

I've come from a rainbow! How do you do?
My color is (name of color)! What color are you?

Join hands with the child, making a rainbow arch. Encourage
that child to choose the next child, and so on . . .

B. Celebrating . . .

Make a colorful, fluttering banner by tacking long pieces of   yardstick/
colored ribbon to a yardstick or tree branch. Hold the banner   branch
while singing the song. Encourage each child to touch and name   ribbons
their favorite color as you repeat the CHORUS.
Use the banner as a fun transition time activity. For exam-   tacks
ple:

Kathy, can you go under the rainbow
and get your coat and mittens?

C. Embracing . . .

Let the children experiment with color mixing! Provide plastic   plastic bowls
bowls of food coloring plus water and paper towels. Show the   paper towels
children how to fold up the towels into squares. Encourage them
to dip their folded paper towels into different colors.   food coloring
Guide the children in squeezing the water out of their towels   water
by pressing them between sheets of newspaper. Unfold the paper   newspaper
towels and observe how the colors combined!

words and music:
Bob Messano

(smoothly)

My Favorite Colors

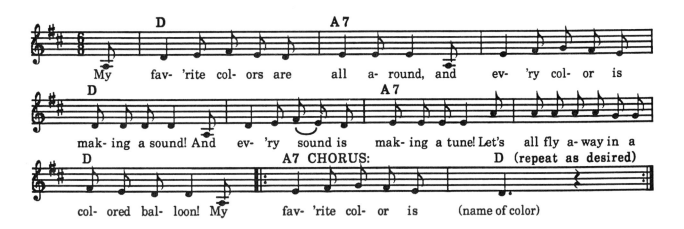

My fav- 'rite col- ors are all a- round, and ev- 'ry col- or is mak- ing a sound! And ev- 'ry sound is mak- ing a tune! Let's all fly a- way in a col- ored bal- loon! My fav- 'rite col- or is (name of color)

2. I roll my colors into a ball,
   I bounce my colors all over the wall!
   My dad comes home and shakes his head . . .
   He picks up the colors and puts them to bed!

   (CHORUS)

3. I put my colors into a box,
   I fasten the lid with chains and locks!
   My mom comes home with a shiny key . . .
   And gives back all of my colors to me!

   (CHORUS)

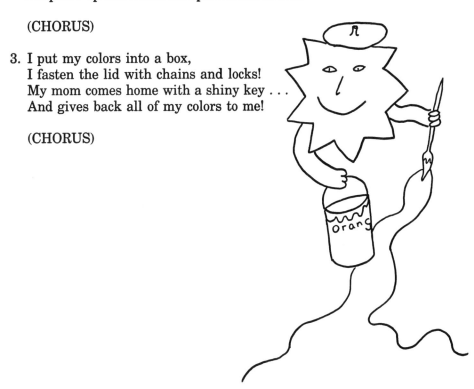

Title: **Nobody Else Is Quite Like Me**

Skills: discusses self and others
identifies body parts
creates nutritious art

Development: Materials:

A. Awakening . . .

Create a bulletin board to display photos of the children at work   camera
and play (at the children's eye-level). Encourage the children to   film
identify themselves and their friends. Ask them to describe what   bulletin board
the people in the photos are doing, what they are wearing, what   push pins
they might be saying, etc.
   Challenge the children to find "look-alikes" in the photos.
For example: someone with the same color hair, a similar expression, etc. Explore differences between people through further
questions.

B. Celebrating . . .

Encourage the children to point to their body parts as they are   stuffed animal/
mentioned in the song.   doll
   For variation, invite the children to hold a stuffed animal or
doll for a "touchable partner." Model a gentle way of touching by
holding a doll yourself as you sing.

C. Embracing . . .

Let the children make a "Veg-a-Buddy!" Provide each child with   paper plate
a paper plate to work on and a variety of vegetables to arrange.   vegetables
For example: carrot and celery sticks, olives without pits, slices of   safety knives
tomato, cucumbers, etc.
   Encourage the children to create head, arms, torso, legs, etc.
Ask them to invent names for their completed characters.
   Invite the children to eat their creations.

32

words and music:
Bob Messano

Nobody Else Is Quite Like Me

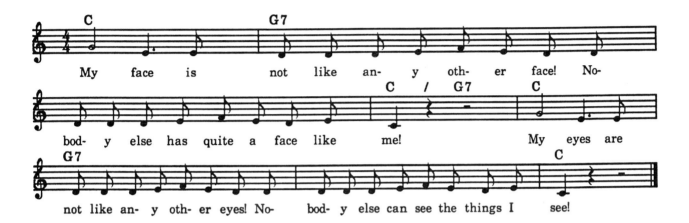

My face is not like an- y oth- er face! No-
bod- y else has quite a face like me! My eyes are
not like an- y oth- er eyes! No- bod- y else can see the things I see!

2. My ears are not like any other ears . . .
An elephant does not have ears like me!
My nose is not like any other nose . . .
It fits into my face so perfectly!

3. My hands are not like any other hands . . .
We've been together for so very long!
My feet are not like any other feet . . .
They're the ones that help me move along!

4. My mouth is not like any other mouth . . .
You should hear the things it has to say!
My brain is not like any other brain . . .
Thinks of things in its own special way!

33

Title: **Our Train**

Skills: enjoys riddles

plays a dramatic role

assembles shapes to form a picture

Development: **Materials:**

A. Awakening . . .

Share the following riddle: words to riddle

> My body's full of people.
> My head is full of steam.
> My tail has got a red light on . . .
> My whistle's like a scream!
>
> What am I? (a train)

Ask the children to imagine what one train might say to another
as they passed along the tracks.

B. Celebrating . . .

Ask the children to form a train by having each child hold onto   none
the waist of the person in front of them. Chant the song as the
train chugs around the classroom. Stop the train in the various
play-areas. Ask individual children what they were doing in each
area (playing, pretending, working, building, singing, reading,
etc.).

    Encourage the children to take turns being the engine (line-
leader) and the caboose (the back of the train).

C. Embracing . . .

Let the children make a group mural based on the following   paper shapes
story: scissors

Once there was a great long train, with a roaring locomotive and a   glue
lot of rattling cars. One day the train was going too fast along a   butcher paper
mountain curve and it crashed! I picked up the pieces and here
they are! (show the children shapes cut from construction paper).
Do you think we can put it back together?

    Provide a large sheet of butcher paper (on which you have
sketched railroad tracks), glue, and shapes. Encourage the children to piece the train together.

words and music:
Bob Messano

Our Train

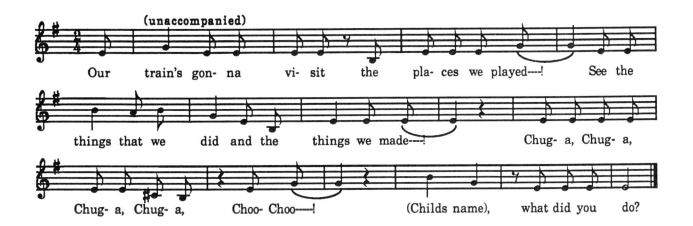

(unaccompanied)

Our train's gon- na vi- sit the pla- ces we played----! See the things that we did and the things we made----! Chug- a, Chug- a, Chug- a, Chug- a, Choo- Choo----! (Childs name), what did you do?

Title: Pick Me Up in an Airplane

Skills: plays imaginatively
moves creatively
constructs a model vehicle

Development:

Materials:

A. Awakening . . .

Bring in a large cardboard box for the children to play in. Cut off
the flaps on top, so they can climb in. Encourage them to use the
box as an imaginary vehicle.

    Provide some props which represent things used by a gas
station attendant. For example: tire pump for gas pump, coffee
can for oil can, plastic tools for real tools, dishtowels for rags, etc.
Encourage the children to service the vehicle.

cardboard box
gas station
  props

B. Celebrating . . .

Gather the children together in a large open space (gym, playground, park, etc.). Encourage them to move around like the
vehicles in the song.

    Adapt the song to include the children's names. For exam-
ple:

(Linda)'s comin' to pick me up in a race car! (3x)
And we'll drive away together!

C. Embracing . . .

Let the children make their own imaginary vehicles! Provide a
variety of recycled materials such as: shoeboxes, egg cartons,
cardboard tubes, coffee can lids, etc. Encourage the children to
assemble the materials with glue, tape or staples.

    Label a table "Our Vehicle Museum." Ask the children to
place their vehicles in the museum so that everyone can look at
them.

recycled
  materials
glue
stapler
tape

36

words and music:
Bob Messano

(playfully)

Pick Me Up in an Airplane

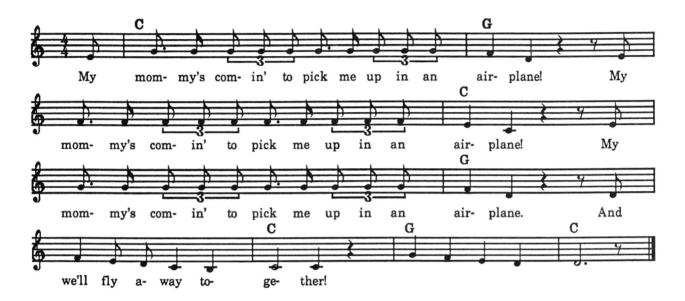

My mom- my's com- in' to pick me up in an air- plane! My

mom- my's com- in' to pick me up in an air- plane! My

mom- my's com- in' to pick me up in an air- plane. And

we'll fly a- way to- ge- ther!

2. My daddy's comin' to pick me up in a speedboat!
   My daddy's comin' to pick me up in a speedboat!
   My daddy's comin' to pick me up in a speedboat . . .
   And we'll zoom away together!

3. My grandma's comin' to pick me up on a skateboard!
   My grandma's comin' to pick me up on a skateboard!
   My grandma's comin' to pick me up on a skateboard . . .
   And we'll roll away together!

4. My grandpa's comin' to pick me up on a rocket!
   My grandpa's comin' to pick me up on a rocket!
   My grandpa's comin' to pick me up on a rocket . . .
   And we'll blast off together! 5-4-3-2-1 . . .

   BLAST OFF!

Title: **Sittin' in a Circle**

Skills: shares space/materials with others
knows the names of classmates
enjoys a tactile art experience

Development:	**Materials:**

A. Awakening . . .

Plan a "Welcome Time" at the beginning of each day at school. Designate a "Circle Area" by making a circle of masking tape on the floor. Place some of the following items inside the circle for the children to explore freely: puzzles, games, small building toys, a "Feely Box" (this is a box whose contents can be felt, but not seen), etc.
    Encourage the children to share and enjoy the materials.

masking tape
puzzles
games
building toys
"Feely Box"

B. Celebrating . . .

Gather the children to "Circle Time" by singing the song. As each child arrives in the circle, ask him or her to name the next child to be chosen. Continue singing until all the children have arrived in the circle.
    Adapt the song for instruments, as follows:

rhythm
   instruments

> *Here we are, sittin' in a circle!*
> *Playin' this song 'til we turn purple!*
> *(Child's name), won't you come and sit with me?*
> *Sit in the circle and play with me!*

C. Embracing . . .

Let the children explore fingerpainting with purple paint! Spread out large sheets of fingerpaint paper on a table. Provide purple fingerpaint for the children to manipulate.
    For variation, add white fingerpaint to the purple and encourage the children to swirl and mix the colors.

fingerpaint
fingerpaint
   paper

words and music:
Bob Messano

Sittin' in a Circle

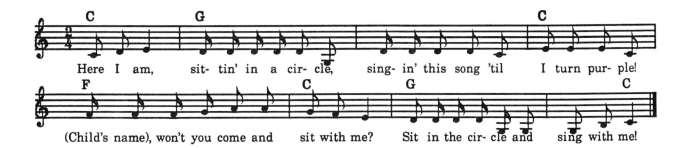

Here I am, sit- tin' in a cir- cle, sing- in' this song 'til I turn pur- ple!

(Child's name), won't you come and sit with me? Sit in the cir- cle and sing with me!

Last Verse: Here we are, sittin' in a circle,
Singin' this song 'til we turn purple!
Purple people like to play . . .
Now it's time to start the day!

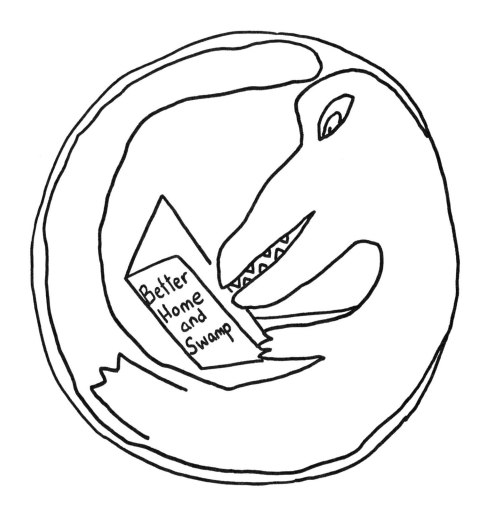

Title: **Sometimes I Feel Happy**

Skills: explore facial expressions in art
expresses emotions through drama
creates a mask

Development:	**Materials:**

A. Awakening . . .

Show the children pictures of masks from various cultures (sources: books, encyclopedias, museums). Ask the children to figure out what kind of expressions the mask-makers are trying to show.
 Point out how the artist exaggerates different parts of the face to express varying emotions.

Materials: pictures of masks

B. Celebrating . . .

Invite the children to make the variety of faces that occur in the song.
 Encourage everyone to clap along to the CHORUS!
 Discuss how important it is to share our feelings in ways which are respectful of the people around us. For example, ask the children if it is better to make an angry face or to hit someone if you feel angry.

Materials: none

C. Embracing . . .

Let the children create their own masks! Provide paper plates for the face and long wooden craft sticks for handles (stapled on by the teacher). Encourage the children to decorate their masks by gluing on a variety of materials, such as: macaroni, beans, buttons, fake hair, yarn, etc.
 Invite the children to use the masks to show their emotions the next time you sing the song.

Materials: paper plates
wooden craft sticks
stapler
glue
assorted art materials

(playfully)

**words and music:
Bob Messano**

Sometimes I Feel Happy

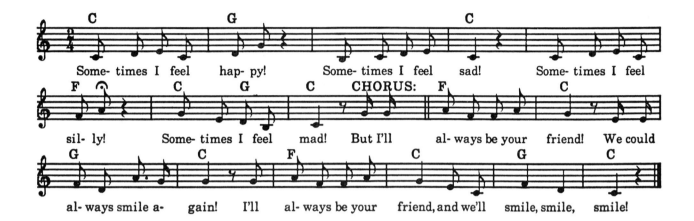

Some- times I feel hap- py! Some- times I feel sad! Some- times I feel sil- ly! Some- times I feel mad! But I'll al- ways be your friend! We could al- ways smile a- gain! I'll al- ways be your friend, and we'll smile, smile, smile!

2. Sometimes I feel sleepy!
Sometimes I feel small!
Sometimes I feel creepy!
Sometimes I feel tall!

(CHORUS)

Title: **Telephone Call**

Skills: plays imaginatively
uses a prop to enliven a song
remembers phone number

Development: **Materials:**

A. Awakening . . .

Place old telephones in the "Family Area" of the classroom. If   old telephones
possible, take apart one of the phones for the children to investigate. Join in the children's conversations as they use the phones
during their play. Encourage them to extend their thinking by
asking creative questions. For example:

Will you meet me at the grocery store today?
What are you wearing to the party?
What are you going to do at the park?

B. Celebrating . . .

Ask the children to play a musical game, as follows: play telephone
Invite the children to sit in a circle. Hold a play telephone
and sing the song to one of the children. Pass the phone around
the circle, singing to each child in turn. Talk to them on the
phone!
If a child answers that he/she is not home, ask him/her
where they are.

C. Embracing . . .

Let the children make a tactile representation of their phone   cardboard
number! Write the children's phone numbers on pieces of card-   dry beans
board. Carefully cover the numbers with glue and provide the   glue
children with dry beans to cover their numbers.   marker
Explain the project to parents and ask them to practice their
phone number with their children on a regular basis.

words and music:
Bob Messano

Telephone Call

I'm call-ing (Child's name) on the tel-e-phone! Ring-Ring! Ring-Ring! Is an-y-bod-y home?

Title: **That Hat**

Skills: enjoys dressing up
marches to music
creates a sculpture

Development: **Materials:**

A. Awakening . . .

Invite the children to a "Hat Day" at school. Ask parents to   hats
provide the children with a hat to wear at school (baseball cap,
engineer hat, hard hat, sombrero, homemade hat, etc.).
　　During "Circle Time," ask each child to tell what kind of hat
he/she is wearing.
　　Play a version of "Simon Says" by making every command
include the word "hat." For example: "*Simon says, put your hat on
your nose!*"

B. Celebrating . . .

Have a "Hat Parade." Encourage the children to do a lively march   same
around the room as you sing the song.
　　Adapt the song by inserting the children's names, as follows
(give each child a turn to lead the parade!):

(Child's name)'s got a hat! It's a very funny hat!
What do you think about that hat?

C. Embracing . . .

Let the children make decorative sombreros! Provide each child   paper plates
with a paper plate and a paper bowl. Guide the children in gluing   paper bowls
the bowl (open-side down) onto the plate. Encourage them to   glue
decorate the hat by tearing strips of colorful crepe paper and   crepe paper
gluing them on.   hole puncher
　　Punch a hole in the hat brim (plate) so the sombrero can be   string
hung on the wall or suspended from the ceiling by a string.

words and music:
Bob Messano

That Hat

I've got a hat! It's a ve- ry fun- ny hat! What do you think a- bout

1. C Fine **2.** C F

that hat? that hat! I wear it in the sun- shine, I

C F

wear it in the rain! I wear it in the kitch- en, I

G Ritardando D.C. al Fine

wear it on the train! Choo! Choo!

Title: **Toys on the Shelf**

Skills: knows where classroom materials are stored
responds to a transition signal
creates a picture book

Development: **Materials:**

A. Awakening . . .

Play a cooperative game, as follows: cardboard box
    Fill a box with play objects from the various learning areas   play objects
of the classroom. Hold up one object at a time and ask the children
if they know where it belongs. Choose one child to put the object
back in its place. Continue until all the children have had a turn.
    Thank the children for helping you!

B. Celebrating . . .

Teach the children the words to the song. Make a tape recording   tape recorder
of them singing it, accompanied by rhythm sticks.   cassette tape
    Play the tape as a transition signal for "Clean Up Time."   rhythm sticks
Encourage the children to help each other put the classroom in
order.
    Adapt the song to new situations. For example:

    Parum! Parum! I'm crawlin' on my knees!
    Parum! Parum! I lost a puzzle piece!

C. Embracing . . .

Let the children make a "Book of Favorite Toys!" Provide pictures construction
of classroom toys cut from school supply catalogs, as well as   paper
pictures of toys from colorful newspaper advertisements or circu- pictures of toys
lars. Encourage the children to paste their favorite toys on a   scissors
series of construction paper sheets. Label the toys with the chil- paste
dren's descriptions.   stapler
    Staple the books together and label them with the children's marker
names. Encourage them to take them home and share them with
their parents and siblings!

(with a strong rhythm)

words and music:
Bob Messano

Toys on the Shelf

Pa- rum! Pa- rum! Toys on the shelf! Pa- rum! Pa- rum! I

did it by my- self!

2. Parum! Parum!
   Dolly's in her bed!
   Parum! Parum!
   A pillow by her head!

3. Parum! Parum!
   Put away the blocks!
   Parum! Parum!
   The people and the trucks!

4. Parum! Parum!
   Moppin' up the floor!
   Parum! Parum!
   My knees are gettin' sore!

5. Parum! Parum!
   Sweep goes the broom!
   Parum! Parum!
   Tidy up the room!

   (repeat first verse)

Title: Up in My Treehouse

Skills: responds to poetry
shows imaginative thinking
enjoys art in the outdoors

Development: **Materials:**

A. Awakening . . .

Share the following poem: paper
marker

> Kristin hammers,
> Leon saws,
> The cat's in the branches,
> Stretching her paws.
>
> The summer wind comes,
> And the summer wind ceases . . .
> Did you ever build a treehouse,
> From old bits and pieces?

Ask the children what sounds they might hear if they were up in
a treehouse. Make a list of their ideas and read it back to them.

B. Celebrating . . .

Ask the children to pretend they are in a treehouse. Choose one   milk crate
child to be the "lookout", by standing on a milk crate. Sing the
CHORUS of the song. Encourage the child to tell everyone what
he/she sees. Adapt the verse of the song, according to their ideas.
For example:

> I see a giant, peeking in the door . . .
> I see a witch, riding by the moon . . .
> I see a star, falling in the sea . . .

C. Embracing . . .

Let the children paint beneath a tree! Set up easels under the   easels
welcoming branches. Provide the children with tempera paint,   tempera paint
paper, and paintbrushes. Vary the colors of the paint according to paintbrushes
the season in your area. For example: paper

Spring: light green, pink, yellow, purple
Summer: green, blue, white, yellow
Fall: orange, red, gold, brown

words and music:
Bob Messano

Up in My Treehouse

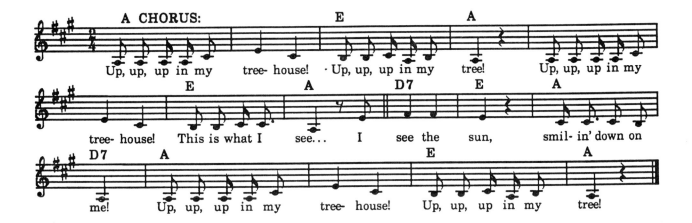

Up, up, up in my tree- house! ·Up, up, up in my tree! Up, up, up in my tree- house! This is what I see... I see the sun, smil- in' down on me! Up, up, up in my tree- house! Up, up, up in my tree!

(CHORUS)

2. I see a bird, singin' just for me!
Up, up, up in my treehouse!
Up, up, up in my tree!

(CHORUS)

3. I see the leaves, dancing in the breeze!
Up, up, up in my treehouse!
Up, up, up in my tree!

(CHORUS)

4. I see my friend, climbin' up to me!
Up, up, up in my treehouse!
Up, up, up in my tree!

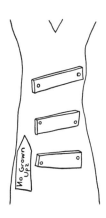

Title: **We'll Be the House**

Skills: creates stories on a flannelboard
plays a cooperative game
cooperates in a group art activity

Development: **Materials:**

A. Awakening . . .

Make a flannelboard available for the children's use in the "Library/Language Area" of the classroom. Provide felt pieces in the shape of family members, pets, and furniture. Encourage the children to create their own "Family Stories" by manipulating and talking about the pieces.

Ask the children to return the pieces to a labeled shoebox. Encourage the children to come up with ideas for other boxes, for example: a zoo scene, an outer space scene, a sports scene, etc.

flannelboard
felt pieces
shoebox

B. Celebrating . . .

Play a cooperative musical game, as follows:

Ask the children to gather around a recreational parachute. Invite everyone to hold onto the edges of the chute. Practice lifting the chute high overhead and letting it descend gently.

Choose a few children to go underneath the parachute while everyone else holds it high. Sing the song while the "family" dances beneath the "roof." Continue until everyone has had a turn.

parachute

C. Embracing . . .

Let the children decorate a playhouse! Provide a large cardboard appliance box with windows and doors pre-cut. Provide tempera paint and paintbrushes for the children to use in beautifying the house.

Set a limit on the number of children who can play in the house when it is complete (two or three at most). Make sure everyone has a fair amount of time to play inside.

appliance box
tempera paint
paintbrushes

words and music:
Bob Messano

We'll Be the House

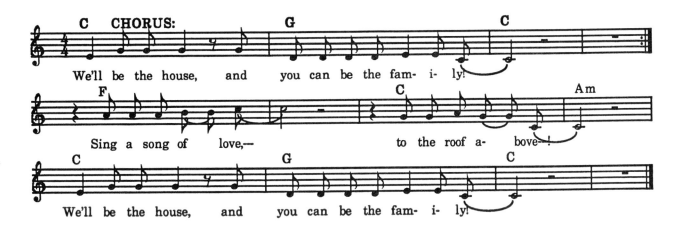

We'll be the house, and you can be the fam-i-ly!

Sing a song of love,— to the roof a-bove—!

We'll be the house, and you can be the fam-i-ly!

2. Ol' rockin' chair, creakin' like a violin!
Ol' rockin' chair, creakin' like a violin!
Sing a song of love, to the roof above . . .
Ol' rockin' chair, creakin' like a violin!

(CHORUS)

3. Springs in the bed, jangle like a tamborine!
Springs in the bed, jangle like a tamborine!
Sing a song of love, to the roof above . . .
Springs in the bed, jangle like a tamborine!

(CHORUS)

4. Listen to the kettle, whistlin' like a flute!
Listen to the kettle, whistlin' like a flute!
Sing a song of love, to the roof above . . .
Listen to the kettle, whistlin' like a flute!

(CHORUS)

Section 2

A Sense of Humor (Music-language arts activities)

This section integrates music and language arts. The songs and activities are particularly suitable for tickling children's love of words and funny situations. Children are encouraged to grow in their capacity to recreate language in joyous ways.

All Mixed Up	*alphabet card spelling*
Barrel Full of Monkeys	*recalling order of events*
The Baseball Boogie	*matching baseball cards*
Bees Buzz	*using descriptive language*
Captain Coconut	*imaginative thinking*
Crazy Weather	*developing pretend situations*
The Elephant Jump	*following game rules*
The Fishy School	*role playing with props*
Frog-a-Phone	*using language creatively*
Happy Blueberry	*following a recipe*
Mr. and Mrs. Mouse	*recalling past events*
My Little Kangaroos	*making comparisons*
No Shoes On	*imaginative play*
Octopus	*exploring puppetry*
Orange, Orange	*categorizing*
Pass Around the Peppermint	*recognizing smells/tastes*
Peanut Butter Pie	*categorizing*
Put Your PJ's On	*oral expression*
Rockin' in the Rabbit Hole	*oral expression*
Scrambled Eggs	*describing actions*
She-Bop	*creative thinking*
The Skunks' Bubble Bath	*sharing experiences*
So Many Bones	*enjoying picture books*
Suzy Turkey	*recreating a sequence*
Tiger at the Movies	*creative puppetry*

Title: **All Mixed Up**

Skills: recognizes letters by sight
responds to a musical signal
spells simple words

Development: **Materials:**

A. Awakening . . .

Make a series of sturdy alphabet cards. Write the letters of the alphabet on squares of cardboard. Cover with clear self-stick vinyl.

oak tag
markers
self-stick vinyl
scissors
stickers

Give each child a card and say the name of the letter as you hand it to him/her.

Play a game where you call out a letter and the child who has that letter trades it in for a sticker. Continue calling letters until all are chosen.

B. Celebrating . . .

Play a musical game, as follows:

alphabet cards

Ask the children to stand in a circle, placing their alphabet cards, letter-side up under their feet. Encourage them to march around the circle of cards while the music is playing and to stop when the music stops.

Sing the song as the children march, stopping at various intervals. Continue until everyone reaches their original letter.

C. Embracing . . .

Play a spelling game with the letter cards, as follows:

same

Choose two or three children to stand up in a row, thereby forming a simple word (hi, dog, cat, etc.). Say and spell the word, as the children repeat after you.

Ask the rest of the children to close their eyes. Mix up the letters by moving the children around. See if someone can make the original word again by moving them back.

(happily)

**words and music:
Bob Messano**

All Mixed Up

All mixed up! All mixed up! How did we get this way?

Walk- in' a- round---- in cir- cles! Got no place to stay!

D.C. al Fine

Title: **A Barrel Full of Monkeys**

Skills: shows imaginative thinking
performs body movements to music
remembers a sequence of events

Development: **Materials:**

A. Awakening . . .

Share the following poem: words to poem

> *Late one night, while the zookeeper slept,*
> *Out of their cages, the monkeys crept.*
> *They climbed in a barrel, and sealed it with glue . . .*
> *A barrel full of monkeys rolled out of the zoo!*

Ask the children to imagine why the monkeys might have wanted
to leave the zoo. Where could they be going? Will they come back?

B. Celebrating . . .

Allow the children to interpret the lyrics by rolling across an exercise mat
exercise mat. Choose a few children at a time to act out the song camera
as you supervise for safety. film
    Ask another teacher or aide to photograph or film the chil-
dren in action. Share the photos with parents and explain the
importance of exercise for young children as a healthy release of
energy.

C. Embracing . . .

Follow up the movement activity by asking the children to recall none
the order of events in the song. For example:

> *Where was the first place the monkeys went?*
>
> *Did the monkeys first go to the mountain or the ocean?*
>
> *Why did the monkeys need a medical kit?*

56

(lively)

words and music:
Bob Messano

A Barrel Full of Monkeys

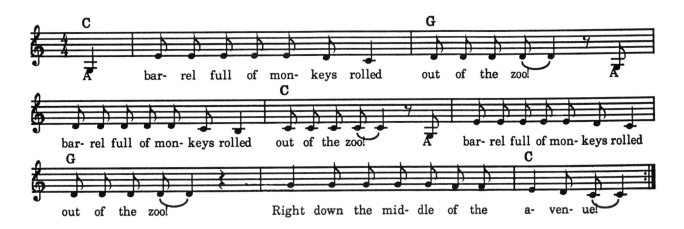

2. They rolled to the ocean and the barrel fell in!
   They rolled to the ocean and the barrel fell in!
   They rolled to the ocean and the barrel fell in . . .
   All the little monkeys had to learn to swim!

3. They rolled to the desert and the barrel was dry!
   They rolled to the desert and the barrel was dry!
   They rolled to the desert and the barrel was dry . . .
   All the little monkeys began to cry!

4. They rolled to the mountain and the barrel was split!
   They rolled to the mountain and the barrel was split!
   They rolled to the mountain and the barrel was split . . .
   All the little monkeys need a medical kit!

5. They patched up the barrel and they rolled along!
   They patched up the barrel and they rolled along!
   They patched up the barrel and they rolled along . . .
   All the little monkeys started singin' this song!

(repeat first verse)

Title: The Baseball Boogie

Skills: enjoys sports
plays a dramatic role
separates things into categories

Development:

Materials:

A. Awakening . . .

Give the children the opportunity to play baseball! Let them take turns using an oversized plastic bat as you pitch them a plastic ball.
For a variation of traditional baseball, show the children how to place the ball atop a traffic cone and hit it while it's stationary. Play the game with a small group so everyone gets to bat frequently.

plastic bat
plastic ball
traffic cone

B. Celebrating . . .

Encourage the children to act out the song, as follows:
Provide half of the children with baseball caps and the other half with pennants (see Appendix, pg. 214). Ask the children with the caps to play the part of baseball players while the other children are the fans.
Sing the song as the players run around the bases and the fans wave pennants and cheer.

baseball caps
pennants

C. Embracing . . .

Let the children enjoy the magic of baseball cards! Bring in a couple of dozen baseball cards and place them in a shoebox. Label the outside of the box with one of the cards covered by a piece of clear self-stick vinyl.
Challenge one or two children at a time to match up the players from the same teams and place them in piles.

baseball cards
shoebox
self-stick vinyl

words and music:
Bob Messano

The Baseball Boogie

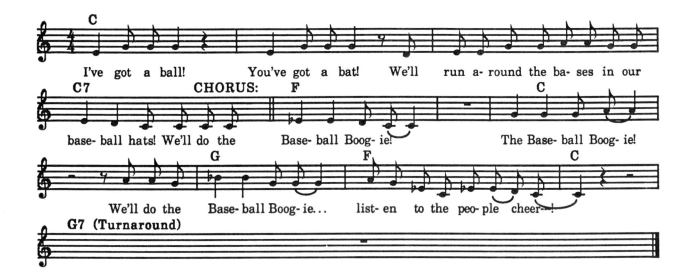

I've got a ball! You've got a bat! We'll run a- round the ba- ses in our

base- ball hats! We'll do the Base- ball Boog- ie! The Base- ball Boog- ie!

We'll do the Base- ball Boog- ie... list- en to the peo- ple cheer—!

2. I hit the ball, it went so high,
   People on the moon saw it passin' by!

   (CHORUS)

3. I ran to first, second and third,
   I'll come home if you say the word!

   (CHORUS)

4. The game's all over, we all had fun,
   Our team lost and the "Grandmas" won!

   (CHORUS)

Title: Bees Buzz

Skills: reads symbols

plays a homemade instrument

uses descriptive language

Development: **Materials:**

A. Awakening . . .

Make a rebus chart with the words to the song (see pg. 215)   oak tag
Substitute simple sketches, photos or labels for the following   markers
words in the song: *bees, butter, bread, honey, head.*   photos/labels
    Encourage the children to read along with you as you point   paste
to the words and pictures.
    Place the chart near the snack table for the children to
discuss.

B. Celebrating . . .

Create a "Bees Band" by letting the children make homemade   cardboard tubes
kazoos. Provide each child with a short cardboard tube, and help   wax paper
him/her fasten a piece of wax paper over one end with a rubber   rubber bands
band. Carefully poke a small hole near the covered end of the tube   pen
using a pen.
    Teach the children to make sounds and music by saying "da-
da-da" into the tube. Invite everyone to "buzz along" to the song.

C. Embracing . . .

Share a "Bees Break" snack with the children! Provide plastic   plastic bowls
bowls filled with honey, honey dippers, and crackers. Encourage   honey
the children to spread the honey on their crackers and taste it.   honey dippers
    Ask the children to describe how the honey looks as it oozes   crackers
off the honey dipper. Tape record the conversation at the snack   tape recorder
table and play it back for the children. Challenge them to identify   cassette tape
their own voices!

words and music:
Bob Messano

Bees Buzz

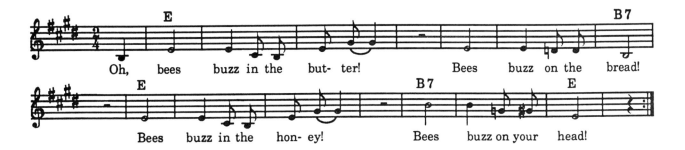

Oh, bees buzz in the but- ter! Bees buzz on the bread!

Bees buzz in the hon- ey! Bees buzz on your head!

2. It's buzz-buzz in the butter!
It's buzz-buzz on the bread!
It's buzz-buzz in the honey!
It's buzz-buzz on your head!

(buzz the melody)

(repeat first verse)

Title: Captain Coconut

Skills: helps make a list
plays a dramatic role
shows imaginative thinking

A. Awakening . . .

Draw a large picture of a suitcase on a piece of paper. Invite the children to go on an imaginary "Sea Voyage." Ask them to help you make a list of things you will need. Draw pictures and/or print their suggestions in the suitcase.

Guide their responses by asking leading questions, as follows:

What will we wear if it's warm on the boat?

What shall we bring to eat?

What will we bring to play with?

paper
marker

B. Celebrating . . .

Invite the children to play the parts of Captain Coconut and his singing shipmates in the song. Provide dress-up clothes fit for sailors, including: red bandanas, sailor hats, raincoats (so'westers), etc. Make a mirror available for everyone to see how they look.

Encourage the children to a sailor's jig (a hopping sort of dance) to the music and to heartily join in singing the CHORUS.

sailor props
mirror

C. Embracing . . .

Gather the children in a circle. Hold a cardboard tube up to your eye and peer through as if it were a mariner's telescope. Share the following poem:

cardboard tube

I'm looking through my telescope,
Far across the sea,
And I see (Captain Coconut) sailing up to me!

Give each child a turn to use the telescope and to describe what they see!

(sea chantey)

words and music:
Bob Messano

Captain Coconut

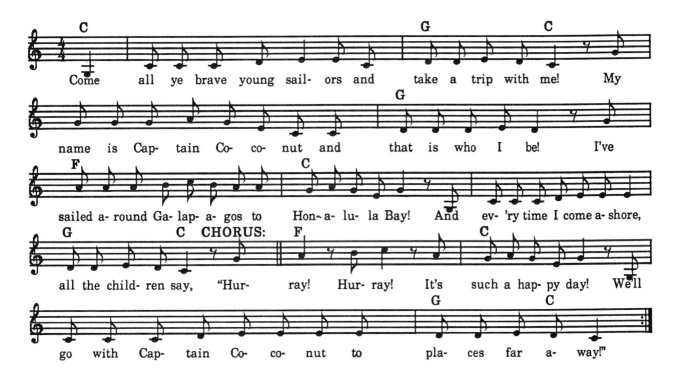

Come all ye brave young sail- ors and take a trip with me! My
name is Cap- tain Co- co- nut and that is who I be! I've
sailed a- round Ga- lap- a- gos to Hon~ a- lu- la Bay! And ev- 'ry time I come a- shore,
all the child- ren say, "Hur- ray! Hur- ray! It's such a hap- py day! We'll
go with Cap- tain Co- co- nut to pla- ces far a- way!"

2. So, bring along your instruments and climb aboard the ship!
The cook is in the galley gettin' ready for the trip!
Right now he is preparing a very special dish . . .
A half-a-pound a' chocolate in a can of tuna fish!

(CHORUS)

3. So, go and tell your mommy where you're goin' to!
I don't want her to worry as you sail the ocean blue!
You won't need your pajamas but you'll need your bathin' trunks . . .
We're goin' to an island inhabited by skunks!

(CHORUS)

(repeat first verse and CHORUS)

63

Title: **Crazy Weather**

Skills: uses symbols to represent events
dances and plays maraccas
develops pretend situations

Development: **Materials:**

    A. Awakening . . .

Make a flannelboard available for the children's use, with felt   flannelboard
pieces representing weather phenomena (sun, clouds, raindrops,   felt pieces
snowflakes, a tree swaying in a strong wind, various items of
dress related to the elements, etc.).
    Encourage the children to help you indicate the day's weath-
er by placing the symbols on the flannelboard.

    B. Celebrating . . .

Encourage the children to dance and play maraccas along to the   maraccas
song!
    Adapt the song to the outdoors by singing the song near a
small hill (monkey bars or other playground climbers can be a
substitute). Encourage the children to climb the hill (pretending
it is the mountain in verse two) and then to come down to the
valley (verse three)

    C. Embracing . . .

Invite the children to use prop boxes filled with dress-up clothes   prop boxes
corresponding to the weather and season. Items in the boxes can   dress-up clothes
include:

    Winter: boots, wool hats, scarves, mittens
    Spring: raincoats, rainhats, spring bonnets
    Summer: sun visors, Hawaiian shirts, flip-flops,
        sunglasses
    Fall: plaid shirts, sweaters, overalls

words and music:
Bob Messano

Crazy Weather

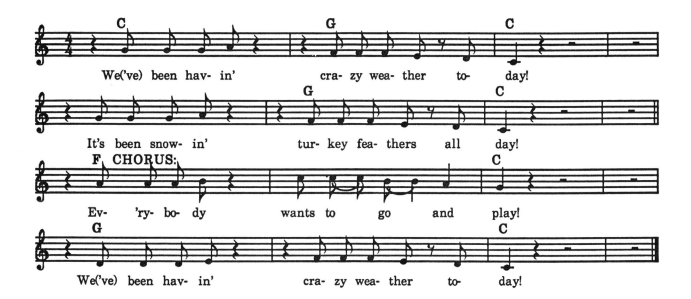

We('ve) been hav- in' cra- zy wea- ther to- day!

It's been snow- in' tur- key fea- thers all day!

CHORUS: Ev- 'ry- bo- dy wants to go and play!

We('ve) been hav- in' cra- zy wea- ther to- day!

2. On the mountain, giants sit and cry!
   All the turkeys have gobbled up the sky!

   (CHORUS)

3. In the valley, dragons make a wish!
   All the turkeys are turning into fish!

   (CHORUS)

   (repeat first verse and CHORUS)

Title: **The Elephants Like to Jump**

Skills: responds to riddles
performs a sequence of body movements
follows rules to a game

Development: **Materials:**

A. Awakening . . .

Ask the following riddle: words to riddle

picture of an
elephant

> *Great floppy ears,*
> *Wrinkles 'round my eyes,*
> *A long, long trunk,*
> *Who am I?* (an elephant)

Show the children a picture of an elephant. Explain that this animal is an endangered species. Ask the children what an elephant might say to people if it could talk.

B. Celebrating . . .

Encourage the children to perform the following movements, as   percussion
suggested by the song lyrics: jumping up and down, shaking the   instruments
entire body, laying down on the floor and pretending to sleep,
jumping again.

For variation, create an "Elephant Band" by giving some of
the children percussion instruments (drums, tamborines, etc.) to
play along to the beat. Ask them to take turns using the instruments and acting out the song.

C. Embracing . . .

Set up a "Feed the Elephant" game for the children to play. Draw   cardboard
an elephant face on a large piece of cardboard. Cut round holes   marker
where the mouth should be. Lean the cardboard against the wall   peanuts
and tape it to the wall and floor.   tape
Give the children whole peanuts to toss at the target, as   scissors
they stand behind a line on the floor. Allow each child five
peanuts to toss. Praise their efforts!

words: Bob Messano
music: trad. "Hat Dance"

The Elephants Like to Jump

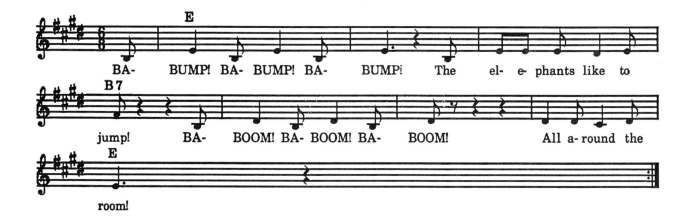

BA- BUMP! BA- BUMP! BA- BUMP! The el- e- phants like to
jump! BA- BOOM! BA- BOOM! BA- BOOM! All a- round the
room!

2. But, when they see a snake,
The elephants start to shake!
They shake and shake and shake,
All around the lake!

They shake and shake and shake,
All around the lake!
They shake and shake and shake,
All around the lake!

3. It's time to go to sleep!
The elephants go to sleep!
It's time to go to sleep!
The elephants go to sleep!

They sleep and sleep and sleep,
The elephants go to sleep!
They sleep and sleep and sleep,
The elephants go to sleep!

(repeat first verse)

Title: The Fishy School

Skills: shows creative thinking
recognizes rhymes
plays imaginatively with props

Development: **Materials:**

A. Awakening . . .

Share the following story: words to story

*Once upon a time, there were some fishies who went to school. They
rode on a fishy school bus and their fishy teacher greeted them at
the door! One day, a whale came to the door of the school and
asked to come in. "I'm sorry," said the teacher, "Our school's too
small for you!"*

Ask the children if they can think of ways to help the whale.

B. Celebrating . . .

Teach the children the words of the song through repetition.   chairs
When they are familiar with the lyrics, ask them to fill in the
rhyming words which you will leave out of the song. Leave out
the following words: *school, whales, apes, down, rats.*
    For variation, create a "Fishy Bus" by making rows of chairs
similar to the seating on a bus. Sing the song as the fishies go to
school. Ask the children what they see out the windows.

C. Embracing . . .

Make a "School Time" prop box available to the children. Include   school props
the following items: small chalkboard, chalk, eraser, bookbags,   prop box
picture books, lunchboxes, pencils, paper, etc.
    Ask the children about their brothers, sisters or friends who
go to school. Encourage them to act out the roles of students and
teachers.

68

words and music:
Bob Messano

The Fishy School

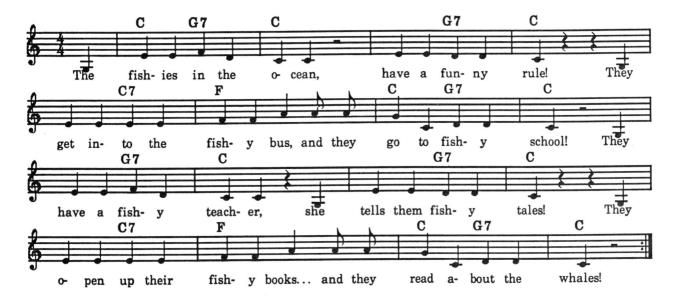

2. The monkeys in the jungle, have a funny rule!
   They get into the monkey bus, and they go to monkey school!
   They have a monkey teacher, she feeds them lots of grapes!
   They open up their monkey books . . .
   And they read about the apes!

3. The bunnies in the forest, have a funny rule!
   They get into the bunny bus, and they go to bunny school!
   They have a bunny teacher, she lets them hop around!
   But if they hop onto her desk . . .
   She tells them to get down!

4. The kitties in the city have a funny rule!
   They get into the kitty bus, and they go to kitty school!
   They have a kitty teacher, her name is Mrs. Cat!
   They open up their kitty books . . .
   And they read about the rats!

Title: **Frog-a-Phone**

Skills: responds to riddles
imitates animal movements
uses language whimsically

Development: **Materials:**

A. Awakening . . .

    Ask the following riddle: words to riddle

> *My legs are green and slimey,*
> *My voice is very deep,*
> *And when I see a fly go by . . .*
> *You oughta see me leap!*
>
> *Who am I?* (a frog)

    Encourage the children to learn the riddle and to share it with
their friends.

B. Celebrating . . .

    Play a musical game, as follows: carpet squares
        Ask the children to pretend they are frogs in a pond. Provide
them with carpet squares to serve as lily pads. Challenge them to
try hopping to a new lily pad, whenever they hear the word "kiss"
in the song (sharing lily pads adds to the fun!).
        Sing the song several times as the children hop from place to
place.
        At the conclusion of the game, ask the children who they
met in the pond.

C. Embracing . . .

    Create a funny "Frog-a-Phone" for the children to explore. Attach   plastic funnels
plastic funnels to both ends of a length of flexible plastic tubing or   plastic tubing/
hose. Tape the funnels to the hose, if necessary.   hose
        Encourage the children to converse with each other by talk-   tape
ing or listening at either end of the phone. Set a time limit on the
use of the phone so everyone gets a turn.

words and music:
Bob Messano

Frog-a-Phone

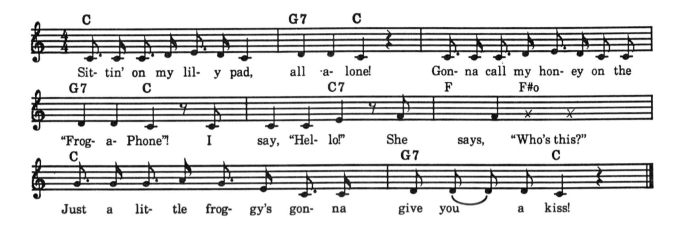

Sit- tin' on my lil- y pad, all -a- lone! Gon- na call my hon- ey on the "Frog- a- Phone"! I say, "Hel- lo!" She says, "Who's this?" Just a lit- tle frog- gy's gon- na give you a kiss!

2. Chompin' on the big flies . . .

3. Croakin' in the moonlight . . .

4. Jumpin' in the water . . .

Title: **Happy Blueberry**

Skills: names things in a category
animates a character in a song
follows a recipe chart

Development: **Materials:**

A. Awakening . . .

Share the following story: words to story

*Once there was a Happy Blueberry who lived on the blueberry
bush. But, one day, somebody came along and picked it! They
put the blueberry into a basket and started to take it home. It was
very dark inside. All of a sudden, the blueberry rolled into somebody . . .*

Who do you think it could have been?

(strawberry, raspberry, cranberry, etc.)

B. Celebrating . . .

Ask the children to pretend that they are as small and round as a   none
blueberry (by rolling their body up into a ball on the floor). Invite
them to pop up when they hear the word "OUCH!" in the song.
For variation, perform the song outdoors where the children
can use their very loudest voices!

C. Embracing . . .

Make a simple recipe chart for the children to follow in creating a   recipe chart
delicious blueberry snack (see Appendix, pg. 216)! Encourage   plastic bowls/
them to follow the pictures on the chart as they pour milk into a   spoons
bowl, add blueberries, and eat it with a spoon. Yum!   milk
Ask the children what other foods blueberries can be added   blueberries
to (cereal, pancakes, muffins, etc.).   measuring cup

words and music:
Bob Messano

Happy Blueberry

I'm a hap- py (blue- ber- ry) Just as sweet as I could be! But,
if you take a bite of me, I might say, "OUCH!"

Ritardando

Variations:

I'm a happy strawberry . . .

I'm a happy raspberry . . .

I'm a happy cranberry . . .

I'm a happy blackberry . . .

(etc.)

Title: **Mr. and Mrs. Mouse**

Skills: interprets pictures

plays a dramatic role

recalls past events

Development: **Materials:**

   A. Awakening . . .

      Place a sign in the classroom announcing, "Mouse Party Today!   oak tag
Please Wear Your Tails!" (for illustration, see Appendix, pg. 217).   marker
      Ask the children to guess what the sign says by looking at
the picture.
      Read the words to them and invite them to the party!

   B. Celebrating . . .

      Play a musical game, as follows: yarn
      Provide the children with pieces of yarn to represent mice/   scissors
cat tails. Fasten the tails to the children with tape. Ask two   tape
children to play the parts of Mr. and Mrs. Mouse while another
child plays the part of the cat.
      Suggest that the cat hide somewhere in the room until it is
time to come out. Sing the song as the children act out the
sequence. Allow other children to join the game.

   C. Embracing . . .

      Hold a "Mouse Party" by serving cheese on crackers at   cheese
snacktime.   crackers
      Repair any tails that may have fallen off during the game!
      Ask the children to recall the events of the game. For exam-
ple:

Which part did you like playing the most?

words and music:
Bob Messano

Mr. and Mrs. Mouse

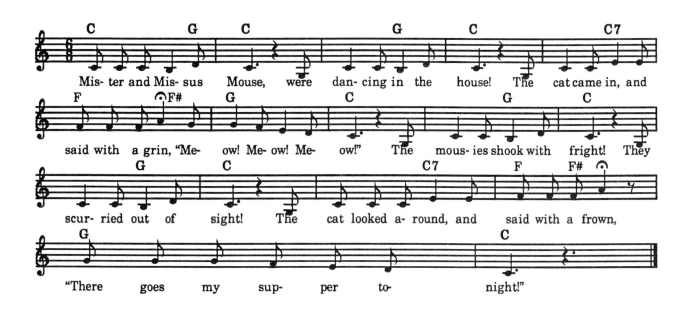

Mis- ter and Mis- sus Mouse, were dan- cing in the house! The cat came in, and said with a grin, "Me- ow! Me- ow! Me- ow!" The mous- ies shook with fright! They scur- ried out of sight! The cat looked a- round, and said with a frown, "There goes my sup- per to- night!"

75

Title: My Little Kangaroos

Skills: shows imaginative thinking
hops to music
makes comparisons; recalls information

Development: **Materials:**

A. Awakening . . .

Show the children a picture of a mother kangaroo with a baby in   mother/baby
its pouch.   animal book

    Ask the children to imagine that they have a pouch (or   paper
pocket) to carry things around in. What sort of things would they
carry?   pen

    Make a list of the children's suggestions and read it back to
them.

B. Celebrating . . .

Create a "Kangaroo Course" in a large space (playroom, gym,   tape/traffic
outdoors). Designate an area for hopping using tape on the floor,   cones
traffic cones, etc.
                                                                       tape recorder
    Encourage the children to hop-along to the song. Praise
their efforts!   cassette tape

    Make a tape of the song for the children to use indepen-
dently.

C. Embracing . . .

Explore books on mother and baby animals. Challenge the chil-   mother/baby
dren to find other animals that carry their young in a pouch,   animal books
other animals that hop, other animals who use long tails for
balance, etc.

    Play a guessing game by closing the book and describing one
of the animals. Let the children take turns searching the book for
the animals.

words and music:
Bob Messano

(playfully)

My Little Kangaroos

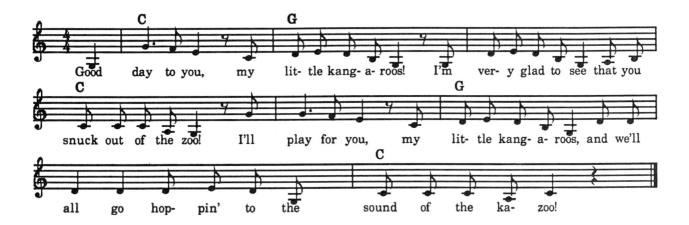

Good day to you, my lit- tle kang- a- roos! I'm ver- y glad to see that you
snuck out of the zoo! I'll play for you, my lit- tle kang- a- roos, and we'll
all go hop- pin' to the sound of the ka- zoo!

2. Mama and the little ones are hoppin' to the beat!
   The baby in the pouch is cryin' for a sweet!
   Don't you cry, my baby, there is some for you . . .
   And we'll all go hoppin' to the sound of the kazoo!

3. Hoppin' through Australia, lookin' all around!
   Koalas in the trees, goannas on the ground!
   All the friendly animals are waitin' here for you . . .
   And we'll all go hoppin' to the sound of the kazoo!

(repeat first verse)

77

Title: No Shoes On

Skills: responds to poetry
performs challenging body movements
plays imaginatively

Development: **Materials:**

A. Awakening . . .

Share the following poem: words to poem

> There's nothing I like more,
> Than to wander by the shore,
> And to dip in the sea with my toes!
>
> With my shoes back home,
> How I love to roam,
> Where the salt wind tickles my nose!

Ask the children to think of things that are fun to do with "no
shoes on" (walking in the grass, standing in a puddle, swimming,
etc.).

B. Celebrating . . .

Play a game, as follows: exercise mat
Let the children take off their shoes and stand on an exer-
cise mat. Challenge the children to try some of the silly ways of
walking described in the song.
Sing the song as the children attempt to walk on their
hands, their knees, their elbows, their bellies, etc.

C. Embracing . . .

Create a "Pretend Shoe Store" in the classroom. Make available a   shoe store props
variety of shoes such as the following: ballerina slippers, hip
boots, high heels, work boots, flip flops, etc. Also, provide items
such as shoeboxes, measuring tape, play cash register and play
money, etc.
Encourage the children to work, shop, and play in the store.
Encourage the children to talk about their own experiences in
shoe stores.

words and music:
Bob Messano

(teasingly)

No Shoes On

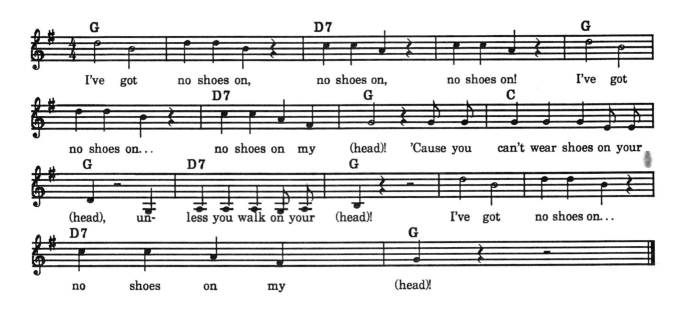

I've got no shoes on, no shoes on, no shoes on! I've got no shoes on... no shoes on my (head)! 'Cause you can't wear shoes on your (head), un-less you walk on your (head)! I've got no shoes on... no shoes on my (head)!

Variations:

I've got no shoes on, no shoes on, no shoes on!

I've got no shoes on . . .

No shoes on my (hands, knees, elbows, etc.) . . .

Title: Octopus

Skills: listens attentively
enjoys a dramatic musical game
explores puppetry

Development: **Materials:**

A. Awakening . . .

Share the following riddle: words to riddle

> *Eight great arms,*
> *Reaching in the sea,*
> *All stuck with suction cups,*
> *Do you know me?*

(an octopus)

Ask the children if they are afraid of octopi. Why?

B. Celebrating . . .

Play a dramatic musical game, as follows: two blankets
    Invite the children to sit on a large blanket. Place another
blanket nearby. Sing the song once to introduce it. Ask the
children to pretend they are the fishies in the song.
    Explain that you are going to play the part of a playful
octopus. Challenge the children to try and swim away from you
when they are chosen. Chant the CHORUS and choose a child.
Catch the fishy and place him/her tenderly on the other blanket
(the Octopus Cave).
    Continue until all the fishies are caught and then pretend to
go to sleep so they can sneak back to their safe blanket.

C. Embracing . . .

Create an "Undersea Scene" in a cardboard box (see Appendix,   cardboard box
pg. 218). Hang strips of colored cellophane from the top (for   cellophane
seaweed) and provide cardboard cutouts of various sea-creatures,   scissors
painted with fluorescent paint.   tape
    Let the children take turns playing with the scene and   wooden craft
cutouts.   sticks
    Turn out the lights and hold a flashlight on the scene while   cardboard
the children move the cutouts.   fluorescent
                                                                             paint
                                                                        flashlight

80

words and music:
Bob Messano

Octopus

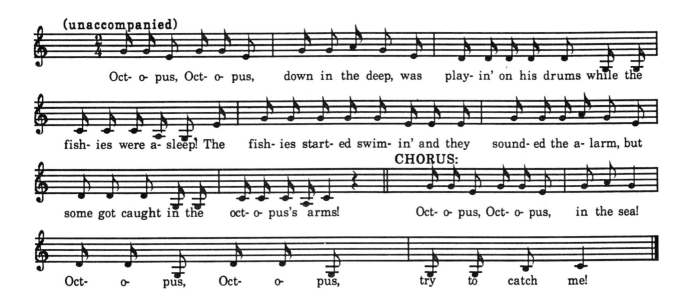

(unaccompanied)

Oct- o- pus, Oct- o- pus, down in the deep, was play- in' on his drums while the fish- ies were a- sleep! The fish- ies start- ed swim- in' and they sound- ed the a- larm, but some got caught in the oct- o- pus's arms!

CHORUS:

Oct- o- pus, Oct- o- pus, in the sea! Oct- o- pus, Oct- o- pus, try to catch me!

Title: **Orange Orange**

Skills: participates in a field trip
plays a dramatic role
names things in a category

Development: **Materials:**

   A. Awakening . . .

       Visit the produce section of a supermarket or neighborhood store! fruit
Involve the children in selecting a variety of fruits which can be safety knife
used to make a fruit salad. bowl
      Take the fruit back to the school and invite the children to
help peel it, slice it with a safety knife, and add it to a large bowl.
      Cover the bowl and refrigerate. Serve it for snack later on in
the day.

   B. Celebrating . . .

       Encourage the children to act out the "falling down" part of the exercise mat
song on an exercise mat or outside on soft, grassy earth.
      For variation, ask some of the children to pretend they are
people from the first aid squad who come to help the fallen ones
get up.
      Trade places and repeat.

   C. Embracing . . .

       Share the fruit salad that you made earlier! Challenge the chil- fruit salad
dren to name the different fruits in their bowl.
      Send home a short newsletter to parents (you can call it a
"Fruit-o-Gram"). Share information about the activity including:
the lyrics to the song, your class recipe for fruit salad, anecdotes
from the field trip, etc.

82

words and music:
Bob Messano

Orange Orange

Or- ange, or- ange, roll- in' down the hill! Rolled all the way to my Unc- le Bill! Unc- le Bill said, "Whoops!" and he fell on the ground! And the or- ange- or- ange went roll- in' 'round!

2. Orange, orange, rollin' by the lake!
Rolled all the way to my Uncle Jake!
Uncle Jake said, "Whoops!" and he fell on the ground . . .
And the orange, orange went rollin' 'round!

3. Orange, orange, rollin' down the street!
Rolled all the way to my Uncle Pete!
Uncle Pete said, "Whoops!" and he fell on the ground . . .
And the orange, orange went rollin' round!

4. Orange, orange, rollin' through the park!
Rolled all the way to my Uncle Mark!
Uncle Mark said, "Whoops!" and he fell on the ground . . .
And the orange, orange went rollin' round!

Title: Pass Around the Peppermint

Skills: responds to poetry
explores puppetry
recognizes smells/tastes

Development: **Materials:**

A. Awakening . . .

Start an indoor edible herb garden! Ask the children to help fill a   soil
planter with soil; plant a variety of herb seeds (including mint);   planter
and take turns watering the plants.   herb seeds
Teach the children the lore of plants. For example, share the   words to poem
following poem:

> A seed needs water,
> A sprout needs light,
> A bud needs a touch of spring,
> To blossom overnight!

B. Celebrating . . .

Invite the children to use a set of stick puppets which correspond   puppet patterns
to the characters in the song (see Appendix, pg. 219).   wooden craft
Sing the song and encourage the children to hold up and   sticks
move the characters as they are mentioned.   crayons
Store the puppets in a box for the children to select indepen-   glue
dently.   box

C. Embracing . . .

Harvest the herbs from your garden! Encourage the children to   herbs
learn to identify the herbs by scent and/or taste.   bandana
Play a game by blindfolding someone with a bandana and
asking them to guess the names of the herbs by smelling or
tasting.
Send home a newsletter to parents about growing experiences they can undertake with their children.

words and music:
Bob Messano

Pass Around the Peppermint

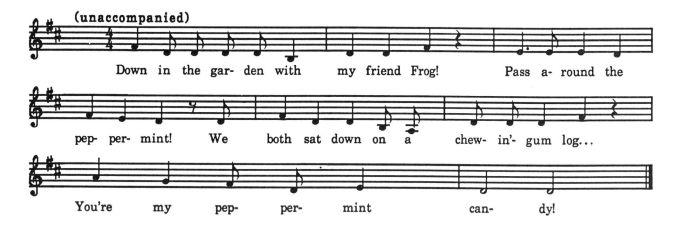

(unaccompanied)

Down in the gar- den with my friend Frog! Pass a- round the pep- per- mint! We both sat down on a chew- in'- gum log... You're my pep- per- mint can- dy!

2. Down in the garden with my friend Snake!
   Pass around the peppermint!
   We both went home with a big bellyache . . .
   You're my peppermint candy!

3. Down in the garden with my friend Snail!
   Pass around the peppermint!
   We both went swimmin' in a waterin' pail . . .
   You're my peppermint candy!

4. Down in the garden with my friend Slug!
   Pass around the peppermint!
   We rode on the back of a big black bug . . .
   You're my peppermint candy!

Title: **Peanut Butter Pie**

Skills: helps create a nutritious snack
plays a game cooperatively
names things in a category

Development: **Materials:**

A. Awakening . . .

Make peanut butter! Invite the children to help shell peanuts and   whole peanuts
remove the skins. Place the shelled peanuts in a large bowl.   vegetable oil
  Measure out peanuts by the cup and place in a blender. Add   bowl
about two tablespoons of vegetable oil for every cup of peanuts   tablespoon
used. Blend until the mixture is smooth and consistent.   measuring cup
  Store in a covered bowl in the fridge.   blender

B. Celebrating . . .

Play a cooperative game, as follows: doctor props
  Ask one or two children to dress up as doctors. Sing the song
as the rest of the children pretend to be stuck. Encourage the
doctors to pull and pry their patients loose!
  For variation, invite the children to be stuck together with a
partner or partners.

C. Embracing . . .

Share the homemade peanut butter on celery sticks, apples, or   peanut butter
crackers! Allow each child to spread their peanut butter using a   celery/apples/
plastic knife.   crackers
  Ask the children if they can name other sticky foods (honey, plastic knives
syrup, molasses, etc.).

(vibrantly)

words and music:
Bob Messano

Peanut Butter Pie

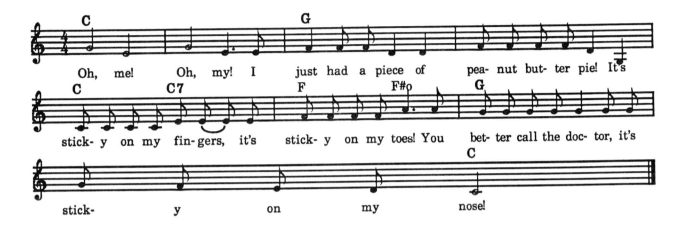

Oh, me! Oh, my! I just had a piece of pea- nut but- ter pie! It's stick- y on my fin- gers, it's stick- y on my toes! You bet- ter call the doc- tor, it's stick- y on my nose!

Variation:

Oh, me! Oh, my!
I just had a piece of peanut butter pie!
It's sticky on my fingers,
It's sticky on my toes . . .
You'd better call the fireman to bring the firehose!

Title: **Put Your PJ's On**

Skills: discusses familiar experiences
adapts a song
describes a favorite object

Development: **Materials:**

 A. Awakening . . .

Make a flannelboard available for the children's use. Provide felt   flannelboard
pieces representing various aspects of bedtime (see Appendix, pg.   felt pieces
220).
Encourage the children to store the felt pieces in a labeled
box (attach a picture of a bed, covered with clear self-stick vinyl).
Ask the children about their favorite bedtime stories, songs,
stuffed animals, etc.

 B. Celebrating . . .

Invite the children to accompany the song by playing tamborines.   tamborines
Encourage them to chant the line, "Put your pj's on!" throughout
the song.
Adapt the song by asking the children what they might say
if they didn't want to go to sleep. For example:

> *Put your pj's on!*
> *My pillow's very rocky!*
> *Put your pj's on!*
> *My bed is made of lead!*

 C. Embracing . . .

Invite the children to bring in a favorite bedtime object (book,   bedtime objects
stuffed animal, blanket, etc.) to "Sharing Time." Gather the chil-
dren in small groups throughout the day to tell about their object.
Ask leading questions, such as:

> *Does your teddy bear like to be cuddled?*

> *What happens in your book?*

words and music:
Bob Messano

Put Your PJ's On!

(unaccompanied)

Put your p j s on! I can't find 'em! Put your p j s on! I

think they ran a- way!

1. (cont.)
   Put your pj's on! I cooked 'em in the kitchen!
   Put your pj's on! I ate 'em yesterday!

2. Put your pj's on! I wanna hear a story!
   Put your pj's on! Remember what you said!
   Put your pj's on! I'm very, very thirsty!
   Put your pj's on! I think I'll go to bed!

Title: Rockin' in the Rabbit Hole

Skills: enjoys storytelling

dances to music

discusses nutritious food choices

Development:	**Materials:**

A. Awakening . . .

Invite the children to pretend to be rabbits crouching down in their rabbit hole.

    Introduce the song with the following story:

It was late one night in the rabbit hole,
And the rabbits were whispering,
Let's play a little rock n' roll!
So they turned on their radio,
And it sounded like this . . .

words to story

B. Celebrating . . .

Invite the children to act out the roles of farmers and rabbits.

    For variation, provide props, such as the following: paper rabbit ears and cardboard carrots (see Appendix, pg. 221). Straw hats can be worn by the farmers.

    Repeat the song several times, allowing the children to perform different roles.

    Store the materials in a labeled prop box for the children to use independently.

rabbit prop
  patterns

paper

cardboard

scissors

crayons

straw hats

prop box

C. Embracing . . .

Invite the rabbits and farmers to share a snack of carrot sticks, celery sticks, and other vegetables admired by people and rabbits.

    Ask the children to name their favorite vegetables, as well as those they are not so fond of. Make a list of the favorites to plan for future snacks.

vegetables

paper

pen

words and music:
Bob Messano

Rockin' in the Rabbit Hole

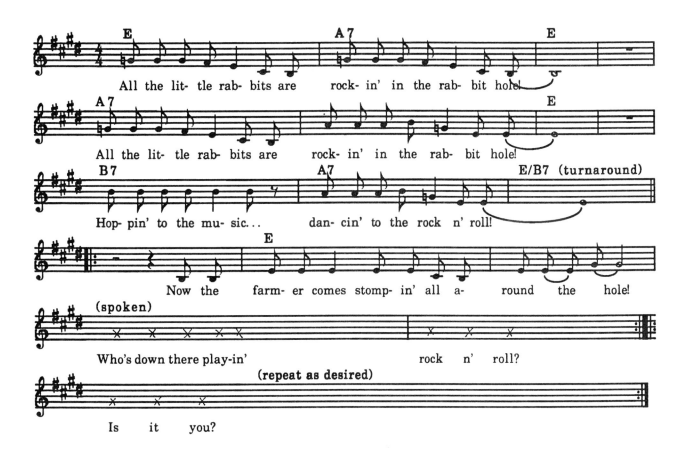

All the lit- tle rab- bits are rock- in' in the rab- bit hole!

All the lit- tle rab- bits are rock- in' in the rab- bit hole!

Hop- pin' to the mu- sic... dan- cin' to the rock n' roll!

Now the farm- er comes stomp- in' all a- round the hole!

(spoken)

Who's down there play-in' rock n' roll?

(repeat as desired)

Is it you?

91

Title: **Scrambled Eggs**

Skills: remembers a sequence
dances to music; plays castanets
describes actions in detail

Development: **Materials:**

A. Awakening . . .

Make a series of five picture cards with the following scenes: a   oak tag
hen laying an egg; a farmer picking up the egg; the farmer   scissors
cracking the egg; the farmer frying the egg; the farmer eating the   markers
egg (see Appendix, pg. 222).
   Set out the cards one at a time on a table, encouraging the
children to describe the sequence of events in their own words.
"Scramble up" (shuffle) the cards and challenge the children to
put them in the original order.

B. Celebrating . . .

Encourage the children to dance along to the music and to act out   castanets
the word "CRACK!" whenever it comes up in the song. Provide
castanets for them to accompany their movements with sounds.
   For variation, try the song with a small group of children
and insert their names into the song. For example:

(Dana) takes the egg and "CRACK!"

C. Embracing . . .

Let the children pretend to make breakfast. Provide the following   cooking props
dramatic play materials in the "Family Area" of the classroom:
empty egg cartons, plastic take-apart eggs, mixing bowl, frying
pan, spatula, whisk, empty salt and pepper shakers, etc.
   Encourage the children to describe what kinds of eggs they
are making (scrambled, over easy, sunny-side-up, poached, bene-
dict, etc.).

(rockin')

words and music:
Bob Messano

Scrambled Eggs

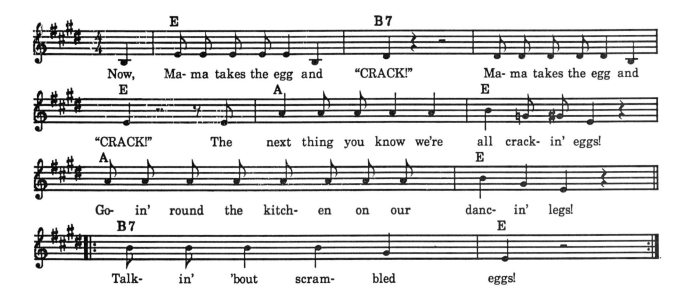

Now, Ma-ma takes the egg and "CRACK!" Ma-ma takes the egg and

"CRACK!" The next thing you know we're all crack-in' eggs!

Go-in' round the kitch-en on our danc-in' legs!

Talk-in' 'bout scram-bled eggs!

Variations:

Now, Daddy takes the egg . . .

Now, Sister takes the egg . . .

Now, Brother takes the egg . . .

(etc.)

Title: **She-Bop**

Skills: understands personal safety
creates props to enhance a song
shows creative thinking

Development: **Materials:**

  A. Awakening . . .

        Read the nursery rhyme "Little Bo Beep."   nursery rhyme
          Ask the children if they know what it feels like to be lost.   book
        Who could they ask for help if they were lost in the following
        places: a supermarket, in their neighborhood, at the beach, at an
        airport, etc.
          Share important safety tips.

  B. Celebrating . . .

        Invite the children to dance and/or play rhythm instruments   rhythm
        along to the song.   instruments
          For variation, encourage them to make and wear costume   grocery bags
        vests cut from paper grocery bags. The children can glue on cotton   glue
        balls for a sheep vest, paint blue for Little Boy Blue's vest, or   cotton balls
        attach bows for Little Bo Peep's vest.   tempera paint
                                                         paintbrushes
                                                         bows

  C. Embracing . . .

        Ask the children to help you to continue the story of Little Bo   paper
        Peep. Follow-up questions could include: marker

            Did the sheep get arrested?

            What happened the next day?

            How could she keep them from running off again?

        Write down the children's responses and read them back later.

94

(bluesy)

words and music:
Bob Messano

She-Bop

Once there was a girl named Lit- tle Bo- Peep! She lived in New York Ci- ty and she had a lot- ta sheep! She took 'em on the sub- way up to Cen- tral Park one day, took out her har- mon- i- ca and start- ed to play! The peo- ple start- ed dan- cin' to the sound of the beat, as the sheep got in a tax- i they were sing- in' so sweet... She- bop! She- bop!

CHORUS:

She- bop! She- bop! She- BAA AAAAAA! She- bop! She- bop! She- bop! She- bop! She- BAA AAAAAA! She- bop! She- bop! She- bop! She- bop! She- BAA AAAAAA!

2. Little Bo Peep was cryin', she didn't know what to do,
She went into a phone booth and called up Little Boy Blue!
He said, don't worry, things'll be alright,
Your sheep'll come back home before the mornin' light!
Sure enough, about the break 'a dawn,
The sheep come in the door and they were singin' that song . . .

(CHORUS)

3. Little Bo Peep had a party, and everyone was there,
She invited Goldilocks and even the Three Little Bears!
Everyone was dancin', and clappin' their hands,
All the little sheep were playin' in the band!
They didn't stop jammin', 'til half-past-five,
When the cops knocked on the door, they said,
"HEY! CUT THAT JIVE!"

(CHORUS)

Title: The Skunks' Bubble Bath

Skills: explores materials related to personal hygiene
uses a prop to enhance a song
shares personal objects/experiences from home

Development: **Materials:**

A. Awakening . . .

Fill the water table (or a large plastic basin) with suds by adding   water table
liquid soap to the water. Provide bath items such as the following: liquid soap
scrub brushes, shampoo bottles, wash cloths, sponges, etc.   bath items
Let the children bathe plastic baby dolls and wash their   baby dolls
hair.
Provide bath towels for the children to dry the dolls.

B. Celebrating . . .

Invite the children to act out the role of the skunks in the song.   plastic blocks
Pretend that rectangular plastic blocks are bars of soap.
Encourage the children to scrub-along to the song.
For variation, let the children choose partners. Ask them to
pretend that one of them is a mother or father skunk while the
other is a baby skunk who needs washing.

C. Embracing . . .

Invite the children to bring in a favorite bath toy for a special   bath toys
"Sharing Time."
Gather the children in small groups during the day to name
and describe their bath toys.
Encourage the children to demonstrate their toys at the
water table.

(sea chantey)

words and music:
Bob Messano

The Skunks' Bubble Bath

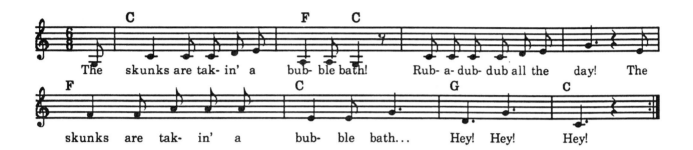

The skunks are tak- in' a bub- ble bath! Rub- a- dub- dub all the day! The

skunks are tak- in' a bub- ble bath... Hey! Hey! Hey!

Variations:

They're scrubbin' up their noses . . .

They're scrubbin' up their whiskers . . .

They're scrubbin' up their tummies . . .

97

Title: **So Many Bones**

Skills: shows curiosity
performs dramatic movements; plays rhythm sticks
enjoys picture books

Development: **Materials:**

A. Awakening . . .

Open up a "Dinosaur Museum!" Place materials, such as the   plastic
following, on and around a table: plastic dinosaurs, wooden dino-   dinosaurs
saur models, dinosaur posters, simulated habitats (a pie pan full   dinosaur models
of water can suggest a swamp, papier-mâché creations can sug-   dinosaur posters
gest a volcanic terrain, etc.).
Encourage the children to touch, play with, explore, and   dinosaur props
question the exhibit.

B. Celebrating . . .

Create hobby-horses with dinosaur heads for the children to take   hobby-head
turns riding. To make the hobby-horses, fasten cardboard cutouts   patterns
of dinosaur heads to dowels (see Appendix, pg. 223). Encourage   cardboard
the children to ride along to the music.
For variation, invite some of the children to play "bones"   markers
(rhythm sticks) while the others ride the hobby-horse. Trade   dowels
places and repeat.   tape
scissors
rhythm sticks

C. Embracing . . .

Visit the children's room of a local library. Arrange with the   dinosaur books
librarian beforehand to pull out a number of picture books featur-
ing dinosaurs. Read one of the stories to the children, then allow
them to browse through the other books.
Help the children select some of the books to borrow for the
classroom.

words and music:
Bob Messano

So Many Bones

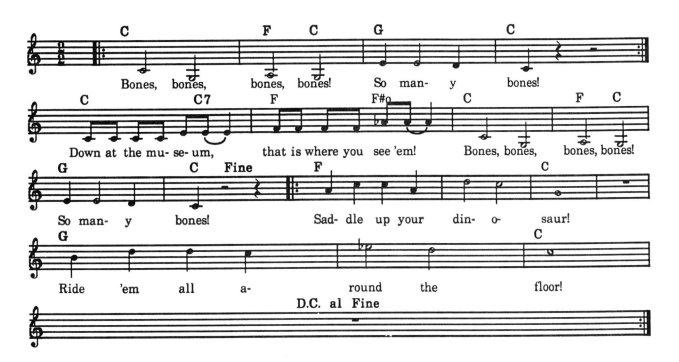

Bones, bones, bones, bones! So man-y bones!
Down at the mu-se-um, that is where you see 'em! Bones, bones, bones, bones!
So man-y bones! Sad-dle up your din-o-saur!
Ride 'em all a-round the floor!
D.C. al Fine

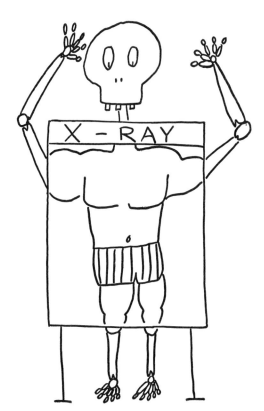

X - RAY

Title: **Suzy Turkey**

Skills: expresses curiosity

plays a dramatic role

re-creates a song sequence

Development: **Materials:**

A. Awakening . . .

Make turkey tracks across the floor of the classroom using colored   self-stick vinyl
self-stick vinyl. (see Appendix, pg. 224). Ask the children to guess   scissors
what kind of animal might have made the tracks. What could it
have been looking for when it came in the classroom?

Show the children pictures of tracks made by other animals.
How are they different?

B. Celebrating . . .

Invite the children to act out the song, by following the turkey   turkey prints
prints on the floor.

Vary the tempo of the music and the dynamics of your voice
to enhance the savory sense of dramatic danger and escape. For
example:

Verse one: moderate tempo; cheerful voice

Verse two: bouncier tempo; playful voice

Verse three: slower tempo; quiet, cautious voice

Verse four: fast tempo; excited voice

C. Embracing . . .

Make "Turkey and Hunter" stick puppets available to the chil-   puppet patterns
dren for their own re-creations of the song sequence (see Appen-   scissors
dix, pg. 224). Provide a tape recorder with a cassette of the song,   crayons
accessible to the puppet stage.   wooden craft
Encourage the children to work the tape recorder indepen-   sticks
dently as they move their stick puppets to the music.   glue

tape recorder

cassette tape

puppet stage

words and music:
Bob Messano

Suzy Turkey

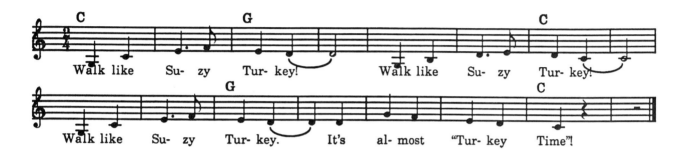

Walk like Su- zy Tur- key! Walk like Su- zy Tur- key!

Walk like Su- zy Tur- key. It's al- most "Tur- key Time"!

2. Flap your wings together!
   Flap your wings together!
   Flap your wings together . . .
   It's almost "Turkey Time"!

3. Tiptoe like a hunter!
   Tiptoe like a hunter!
   Tiptoe like a hunter . . .
   It's almost "Turkey Time"!

5. Run like Suzy Turkey!
   Run like Suzy Turkey!
   Run like Suzy Turkey . . .
   It's almost "Turkey Time"!

Title: **Tiger at the Movies**

Skills: responds to poetry
plays a dramatic role
interprets song through puppetry

Development: **Materials:**

A. Awakening . . .

Share the following poem: words to poem

> *The tiger said to the tailor,*
> *I'm looking for a suit.*
> *Something that the hunters,*
> *Wouldn't dare to shoot.*
>
> *The tailor said to the tiger,*
> *I'll make it jungle green,*
> *And that is why the tiger,*
> *Is seldom to be seen!*

Ask the children what sounds peculiar about this tale.

B. Celebrating . . .

Set up chairs in rows, similar to a movie theater. Help the chil- chairs
dren pair off into partners as they sit in the movie seats. Ask
them to take turns pretending to be friendly tigers and people.
 Sing the song as the children interpret the lyrics dramatically.

C. Embracing . . .

Let the children make their own movie! Set up a projector or lamp projector/lamp
to shine light on a screen or wall. Provide the children with stick movie screen
puppets that represent some of the characters in the song (see puppet patterns
Appendix, pg. 225). crayons
 Encourage the children to create their own interpretations scissors
and stories by performing a "shadow play" with the puppets. wooden craft
 sticks
glue

words and music:
Bob Messano

Tiger at the Movies

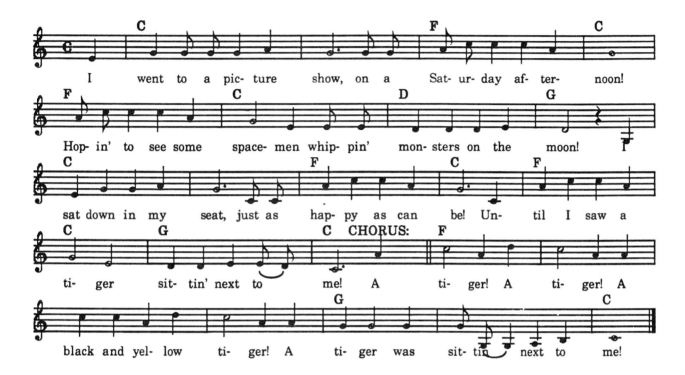

I went to a pic-ture show, on a Sat-ur-day af-ter-noon!

Hop-in' to see some space-men whip-pin' mon-sters on the moon!

sat down in my seat, just as hap-py as can be! Un-til I saw a

ti-ger sit-tin' next to me! A ti-ger! A ti-ger! A

black and yel-low ti-ger! A ti-ger was sit-tin' next to me!

2. He was lookin' hungry, he was lookin' mad,
So I gave him all the candy and the popcorn that I had!
He put his arm around me, his big paw on my knee . . .
Oh, what am I gonna do? There's a tiger sittin' next to me!

(CHORUS)

3. We watched a double feature, I sat right in his lap,
It was so warm and comfy, I took a little nap!
But when the show was over, and all the lights came on . . .
I looked 'round for the tiger, but you know, he was gone!

(CHORUS)

Section 3

A Sense of Wonder (Music-science activities)

This section integrates music and science. The songs and activities are particularly suitable for engaging children's curiosity. Children are encouraged to grow in appreciation and understanding of the world's working processes.

All the Green Things	*sprouting seeds*
Autumn Is Coming to Town	*observing changes over time*
Betsy Bear	*animal habitats*
Boat on a River	*discovering useful natural materials*
Christine the Cat	*sounds in the environment*
The Circus Horses	*parts of a horse*
Cuckoo Clock	*following a time line*
The Day the Snowflakes Danced	*exploring gravity*
Evenin' Star	*naming celestial objects*
The Good Construction Worker	*using tools*
Helicopter	*discovering a nature-made toy*
I Don't Wanna Be Extinct	*dinosaurs*
I'm a Little Birdy	*identifying birds*
I've Got a Big Plane	*field trip observations*
It Looks Like a Unicorn	*growing vegetables*
Little Flower	*observing plant growth*
The Mud Song	*exploring mud*
Put Your Ear to a Seashell	*exploring fossils*
The Rainbow Sea	*exploring wave formation*
The Snow	*weather conditions*
Time to Listen	*animal adaptation*
The Tree's Song	*exploring a mini environment*
Up in the Pine Cone Tree	*making a bird feeder*
We're in a Spaceship	*imaginative play*
Why Do the River Go Up?	*experimenting with bubbles*

Title: **All the Green Things**

Skills: uses descriptive language
plays a cooperative game
enjoys growing things

Development: **Materials:**

A. Awakening . . .

Send home a note to parents, asking them to help their child find   note to parents
a green object or living thing to bring in for "Sharing Time."
Provide a place for the children to keep their objects during the
day, such as a table, basket, or box.
Give each child the opportunity to name and describe their
object. Help them to express themselves by asking leading questions, for example:

What kind of tree did these leaves come from?

B. Celebrating . . .

Invite the children to play a cooperative musical game, as follows: green oak tag
Let each child choose and wear a necklace with a green   scissors
character (see Appendix, pg. 226), corresponding to the verses of
the song. Encourage everyone to join hands in a circle with their   marker
fellow "green things" as they are mentioned.   hole puncher
Sing the song as the children dance and all the characters   string
become part of the circle.

C. Embracing . . .

Invite the children to participate in the miracle of sprouting   sprout seeds
seeds! Give each child a few seeds to place inside a transparent   container
container. Place cheesecloth over the mouth of the container and
fasten it with a rubber band.   cheesecloth
Let the children take turns filling the container three-   rubber band
quarters full of water each day, then shaking the water out.
Encourage them to observe the growth of the seeds over the
course of a week. Invite everyone to taste the sprouts at "Snack
Time."

(affectionately)

words and music:
Bob Messano

All the Green Things

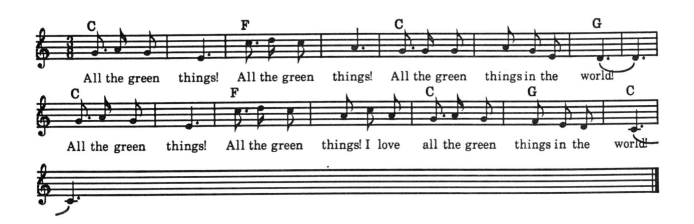

All the green things! All the green things! All the green things in the world!

All the green things! All the green things! I love all the green things in the world!

Variations:

All the green fish . . .

All the green frogs . . .

All the green trees . . .

All the green bugs . . .

(etc.)

Title: **Autumn Is Coming to Town**

Skills: makes observations about leaves
acts out a song sequence with body movements
observes changes over time

Development: **Materials:**

A. Awakening . . .

Collect autumn leaves and arrange them on a table in your   leaves
"Science/Discovery Area." Provide a magnifying glass for the   magnifying
children to examine them. Guide them in safely holding the   glass
leaves up to a table lamp to observe the veins inside.   table lamp
    Take a field walk with the children and invite them to
collect leaves. Encourage them to bring some back to the classroom to examine them.

B. Celebrating . . .

Invite the children to act out the song. Suggest that they move   leaves
like leaves being gently tossed in the wind (hand movements or
whole body movements can be performed).
    For variation, perform the song outdoors, using leaves for
hand-held props.
    Ask the children how the song makes them feel.

C. Embracing . . .

Set up the following experiment: basin
    Fill a plastic basin with water and place a variety of leaves water
nearby. Ask the children if they think the leaves will float or sink leaves
if they are placed in the water. Why or why not? Put a few leaves paper
in the water.   marker
    Ask the children to check on the leaves throughout the day.
What changes occur over time? Write down the children's observations and read them back.

(mournfully)

words and music:
Bob Messano

Autumn Is Coming to Town

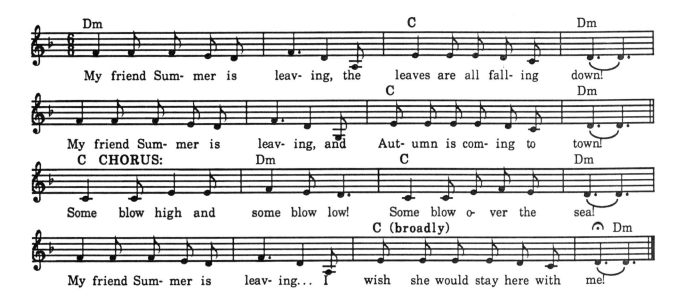

My friend Sum- mer is leav- ing, the leaves are all fall- ing down!

My friend Sum- mer is leav- ing, and Aut- umn is com- ing to town!

CHORUS: Some blow high and some blow low! Some blow o- ver the sea!

My friend Sum- mer is leav- ing... I wish she would stay here with me!

2. Squirrels are gathering acorns,
Storing them up in the trees!
Pumpkins glow in the full moon,
Children play in the leaves!

(CHORUS)

3. Crows are barking a sing-song,
A cold wind rustles the wood!
The leaves are turning to crimson,
A sign of everything good!

(CHORUS)

4. The bees are disappearing,
Into a hollow tree!
The streams are filling with color,
A golden melody!

(CHORUS)

Title: Betsy Bear

Skills: responds to poetry
plays a dramatic game
matches animals to habitat

Development: **Materials:**

A. Awakening . . .

Share the following poem: words to poem

> *Bear and Mouse share a house,*
> *When Earth is cold and gray.*
> *They snuggle down, all safe and sound,*
> *'Til winter goes away!*

Ask the children if it would be a good idea for people to hibernate
in the winter. What would we miss if we slept all winter? (skat-
ing, holidays, sleigh riding, hot cocoa, etc.)

B. Celebrating . . .

Invite the children to play a dramatic musical game, as follows: cymbal
    Ask the children to take turns playing the parts of sleeping
bears and creeping mice. Designate an area, such as your "Circle
Time" rug, as the bears' cave. Suggest a hiding place for the mice.
    Encourage the mice to sneak around the cave; to pretend to
eat cookies; and to scurry off to safety when they knock over the
cookie jar (clang a cymbal for a sound-effect signal).

C. Embracing . . .

Make a hands-on bulletin board at the children's level. Title it: bulletin board
"Animals Who Hibernate" (see pg. 227). Create a scene with a   Velcro™ strips
hollow tree, a cave, a burrow, etc. Place Velcro™ strips in those   cardboard
places and on the backs of the animals who hibernate there.   animal
    Show the children nature books which depict hibernating   cutouts
animals. Invite them to match up the animals at the bulletin
board with the places where they hibernate.

(lullaby)

words and music:
Bob Messano

Betsy Bear

(unaccompanied)   CHORUS:

Don't you wake up,   Bet- sy Bear!   Don't you wake up,   Bet- sy Bear!

Don't you wake up,   Bet- sy Bear!   'Til the win- ter is   o- ver!

2. Little mice come creepin' in!
   Little mice come creepin' in!
   Little mice come creepin' in . . .
   Lookin' for their supper!

   (CHORUS)

3. We'll take some cookies from the jar!
   We'll take some cookies from the jar!
   We'll take some cookies from the jar . . .
   Oops, we knocked it over!

Title: **Boat on a River**

Skills: responds to poetry
dramatizes lyrics
explores uses of natural materials

Development: **Materials:**

A. Awakening . . .

Share the following poem: words to poem

> *Tugboats and barges, sloops with tall sails,*
> *Smiling sailors who stand at the rails.*
> *Sleek-skinned otters, their noses held high . . .*
> *This is our river, may it never run dry!*
>
> *Paddlewheel steamers, birchbark canoes,*
> *People in rowboats, out for a cruise.*
> *Nine baby ducklings, just learning to fly . . .*
> *This is our river, may it never run dry!*
>
> *Folks at the dockside, sinking their bait,*
> *The old navigator, asleep on a crate.*
> *Children with breadcrumbs, clouds drifting by . . .*
> *This is our river, may it never run dry!*
>
> *Tires and bottles, styrofoam cups,*
> *A few good people who clean it all up.*
> *Pete plays his banjo, gulls trace the sky . . .*
> *This is our river, may it never run dry!*

Ask the children to name things that might be seen along a river.

B. Celebrating . . .

Invite the children to move to the music. Provide them with   sailors' hats
sailors' hats and encourage them to pantomime steering the
ship's wheel.
   For variation, sing the song while the children play in a
rocking boat or on a see saw. Encourage them to describe what
they see on their voyage.

C. Embracing . . .

Set up the following experiment: water table
   Fill a plastic basin or water table with water. Let the chil-   tree bark
dren explore the buoyancy of tree bark.
   Discuss how Native Americans and pioneers used birch
bark to make canoes.
   What else could tree bark be used for? (roofs of houses,
paper, drinking cups, etc.)

(flowing)

words and music:
Bob Messano

Boat on a River

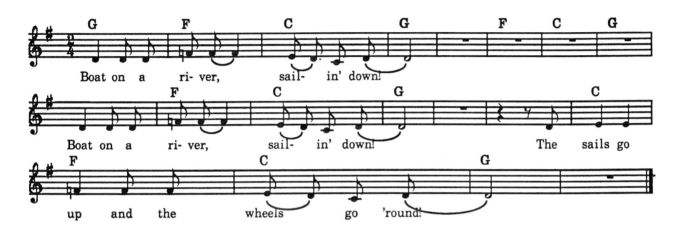

Boat on a ri- ver, sail- in' down!

Boat on a ri- ver, sail- in' down! The sails go

up and the wheels go 'round!

2. Wind is singin', the sails are full!
   Wind is singin', the sails are full!
   There's knots to tie and ropes to pull!

3. Captain, Captain, look around!
   Captain, Captain, look around!
   Tell your shipmates what you've found!

   (repeat first verse)

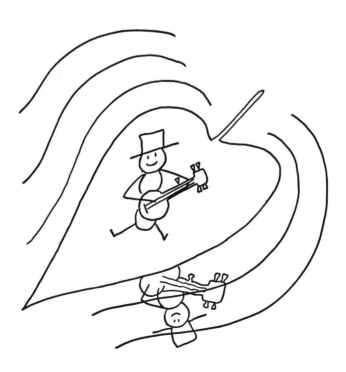

Title: **Christine the Cat**

Skills: shows imaginative thinking
makes sound effects with cymbals
identifies sounds in the environment

Development:

Materials:

A. Awakening . . .

Introduce the song with the following story:

Once there were some little mice who liked to go to the beach. One day, while they were swimming, they saw a beautiful sailing ship heading their way. But as it got closer, they saw that Christine the Cat was at the wheel.

Suddenly, dark clouds moved over the sea. The wind went, "WOOOO!," the thunder went "KABOOM!," and all the little mice just clapped their hands.

What do you think happened to Christine the Cat?

words to story

B. Celebrating . . .

Invite the children to dramatize the song using hand and/or body movements, and by making sound effects. For example, encourage them to move like Christine the Cat's airplane with arms outstretched like wings.

Add instruments to the interpretation. For example, cymbals can evoke the sound of crashing thunder. Let the children take turns using the instruments and moving dramatically.

cymbals

C. Embracing . . .

Borrow a sound effects record from the library or make your own recording of everyday sounds (footsteps, a car starting, a barking dog, children at a playground, etc.). Let the children take turns wearing headphones and guessing the sounds.

Take a field walk and make a list of the sounds that the children hear.

record player
sound effects
record
or
tape recorder
cassette tape
headphones
paper
pen

114

(dramatically)

words and music:
Bob Messano

Christine the Cat

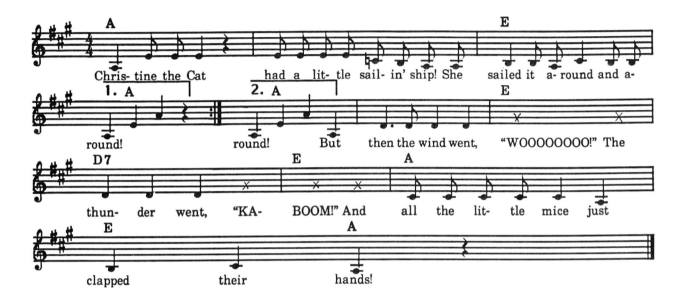

Chris- tine the Cat had a lit- tle sail- in' ship! She sailed it a- round and a-

round! round! But then the wind went, "WOOOOOOOO!" The

thun- der went, "KA- BOOM!" And all the lit- tle mice just

clapped their hands!

Variations:

Christine the Cat had a little airplane!
She flew it around and around . . .

Christine the Cat had a little motorcycle!
She rode it around and around . . .

Christine the Cat had a little balloon!
She floated around and around . . .

(etc.)

115

Title: # The Circus Horses

Skills: responds to poetry
performs galloping, jumping movements
enjoys field trips; names parts of a horse's body

Development: **Materials:**

A. Awakening . . .

Share the following poem: words to poem

> All day long, the people wait,
> Lining the streets of town.
> The dusty distance comes alive,
> With faint, familiar sounds . . .
>
> The clippety-clop of hoofbeats,
> The giggles of a clown,
> The people cheer, 'cause every year . . .
> The circus comes to town!

Ask the children to name things that might pass by in a circus parade.

B. Celebrating . . .

Make a set of "Circus Horse Bells" for the children to wear.   nylon cord
Thread pieces of colorful nylon cord through large jingle bells scissors
(available in craft stores). Knot the cord at a comfortable length jingle bells
for the children to wear like a necklace.   blocks
    Set up some wooden blocks to resemble a low fence. Challenge some of the children to play the part of the galloping, jumping circus horses while the others sing and cheer them on. Trade places and repeat.

C. Embracing . . .

Take a field trip to a stable, farm, mounted-police barracks, etc, to camera
observe horses. Ask a handler to identify the parts of a horse for film
the children. Encourage them to make comments and ask questions.
    Take photos of the children's visit and display them on a bulletin board. Challenge the children to name the parts of a horse (mane, tail, hooves, etc.).

(square dance feeling)

words and music:
Bob Messano

The Circus Horses

The Cir- cus Hor- ses come to town! All the bells are ring- in'! The

Cir- cus Hor- ses come to town! All the bells are ring- in'! Gid- dy

up! Gid- dy up! Gid- dy up! Gid- dy up! List- en to the peo- ple sing- in'! Gid- dy

up! Gid- dy up! Gid- dy up! Gid- dy up! List- en to the peo- ple sing- in'!

Title: **Cuckoo Clock**

Skills: responds to poetry
marches to music
follows a time-line of activities

Development: **Materials:**

A. Awakening . . .

Share the following poem while snapping fingers in time: words to poem

> *Early in the morning the alarm clock rings,*
> *Grandfather chimes and the cuckoo sings.*
> *The pocket watches are wound up tight,*
> *The digital watches are shinin' bright.*
>
> *The old church clock is turnin' slow,*
> *The clock in the kitchen says, "Time to go!"*
> *There's trains to catch and hills to climb . . .*
> *Everybody's movin' to the tick-tock time!*

Ask the children what kind of clocks they have at home.

B. Celebrating . . .

Invite some of the children to tap tone blocks or rhythm sticks in   tone blocks
time to the song. Ask the rest of the children to march along to   rhythm sticks
the music. Trade places and repeat.   masking tape
    For variation, make the numbers of a clockface (1 to 12) on
the floor of the classroom using masking tape. Invite the
marchers to follow the numbers. Stop the song at different intervals and ask the children to name the numbers they are standing
on.

C. Embracing . . .

Make a time-line corresponding to your daily activities (see pg.   computer paper
228). Place clock faces with the various times of day over the   marker
symbols for the activities. Hang an easy-to-read clock (with   clock
hands!) near the time-line for the children to compare.
    Ask the children to help figure out the order of the day's
activities by using the time-line.

words and music:
Bob Messano

Cuckoo Clock

Tick- tock! The clock goes 'round! Ev- 'ry- bo- dy's march- in' to the sound!

Coo- Coo! The lit- tle bird sings! Now it's time to spread our wings!

2. Cuckoo lives in a little square house!
   Most of the time she's quiet as a mouse!
   Never was a bird who took so long!
   Just to sing one little-bitty song!

   (CHORUS)

3. I hear a chirpin' noise inside!
   All of a sudden, the door swings wide!
   Who in the world should I happen to see?
   Pretty little cuckoo lookin' at me!

   (CHORUS)

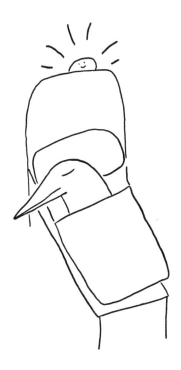

Title: The Day the Snowflakes Danced

Skills: responds to riddles
plays a cooperative game
explores gravity

Development: **Materials:**

A. Awakening . . .

Ask the following riddle: words to riddle
paper
marker

> *I was born in a cloud,*
> *But I look like a star.*
> *I am soft, I am cold,*
> *I will fall very far!*
>
> *What am I?* (a snowflake)

Ask the children to name as many words as they can with the
word "snow" in them (snowball, snowman, snowplow, snow-
shovel, snowcone, snowstorm, etc.) Make a list and read it back to
them.

B. Celebrating . . .

Play a cooperative game, as follows: none
Choose two children to play the parts of the snowflakes in
the song. Ask the rest of the children to pretend to be snowflakes
who have already fallen and are stuck to the ground.
Suggest that the two little snowflakes gently tap their
friends to help them rise up and dance. Trade places and repeat.

C. Embracing . . .

Set up the following experiment: sand table
Fill a large basin or empty sand table with confetti. Invite   confetti
the children to create a snowstorm by sprinkling the confetti   pouring props
using a variety of props, such as: funnel, measuring cup, plastic   plastic farm
spoon, sieve, etc.   animals
Add plastic farm animal figures to the play and challenge
the children to make a winter scene.

120

(calypso)

words and music:
Bob Messano

The Day the Snowflakes Danced

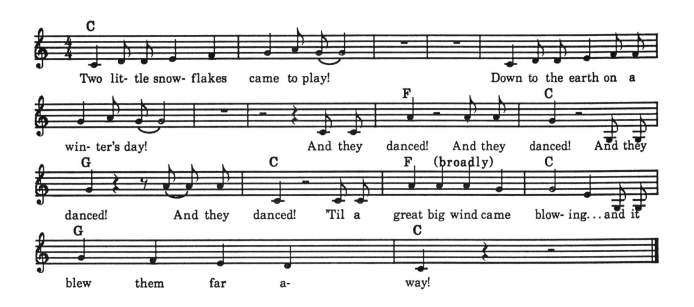

Two lit- tle snow- flakes came to play! Down to the earth on a win- ter's day! And they danced! And they danced! And they danced! And they danced! 'Til a great big wind came blow- ing... and it blew them far a- way!

Title: Evenin' Star

Skills: contributes to story development
plays a dramatic role
names celestial objects

Development: **Materials:**

A. Awakening . . .

Introduce the song with the following story: words to story

*Once there was a wizard who wore a magic hat. It was decorated
with silver stars and a golden moon, and all the planets were there
too!*
    *It seems that this wizard was afraid of the dark, so every
night he cast a magic spell and . . .*
    What do you think happened?

Ask the children to continue the story!

B. Celebrating . . .

Play a dramatic game, as follows: wizard hat
    Let the children take turns pretending to be the wizard in   magic wand
the story. The wizard can wear a magic hat and wield a magic   star stickers
wand. Invite the rest of the children to make a circle around the
wizard and to move to the music.
    Give all the children star stickers to wear on their hands
when the game is finished.

C. Embracing . . .

Create your own classroom planetarium! Let the children deco-   cardboard
rate pre-cut cardboard shapes of celestial objects (stars, moons,   glitter
planets, comets, etc.). with glitter and glue, or fluorescent paint.   glue
Punch holes in their creations and suspend from the ceiling with   fluorescent
fishing line.   paint
    Provide cardboard tubes to act as telescopes. Challenge the   paintbrushes
children to search the "night sky."   hole puncher
                                                                       fishing line
                                                                       cardboard tubes
                                                                       scissors

122

(bluesy)

**words and music:
Bob Messano**

Evenin' Star

Eve- nin' Star, walk a- round the moon, Eve- nin' Star! Eve- nin' Star,

walk a- round the moon, Eve- nin' Star! Eve- nin' Star,

walk a- round the moon, all of the plan- ets will come a- long soon...

Shine your light on me!

2. Evenin' Star, glowin' in the night, Evenin' Star!
   Evenin' Star, glowin' in the night, Evenin' Star!
   Evenin' Star, glowin' in the night,
   All of the planets are feelin' alright . . .
   Shine your light on me!

3. Evenin' Star, twinkle in the dawn, Evenin' star!
   Evenin' Star, twinkle in the dawn, Evenin' star!
   Evenin' Star, twinkle in the dawn,
   All of the planets are singin' that song . . .
   Shine your light on me!

Title: **The Good Construction Worker**

Skills: identifies objects by touch
plays rhythm instruments
uses tools safely and constructively

Development: **Materials:**

A. Awakening . . .

Play a guessing game with a small group of children, as follows: tools
    Ask the children to close their eyes while you place a tool   bandana
(hammer, screwdriver, wrench, etc.) underneath a bandana. Let
them take turns trying to guess what the objects are by putting
their hand on top of the bandana and feeling the shape of the
object underneath.
    When all the objects have been guessed, ask the children
what kind of workers might use such tools (carpenter, roofer,
plumber, etc.).

B. Celebrating . . .

Invite the children to hammer along to the song by playing   rhythm sticks
rhythm sticks. Ask them to listen carefully in the song for the   construction
word "stop" and to stop their work when they hear it.   worker props
    Enhance the action by providing construction worker dress-
up props, such as the following: hard hats, tool belts, plastic tools,
toolbox, etc.

C. Embracing . . .

Set up a workbench in the classroom. Discuss safety rules and   workbench
procedures with the children before allowing them to use it. Also, tools
oversee their work in the beginning to remind them of safe   wood
practices.   accessories
    Invite the children to work with wood and other materials at
the workbench. Encourage all their experiments and efforts,
rather than emphasizing a finished product.

(bluesy)

**words and music:
Bob Messano**

The Good Construction Worker

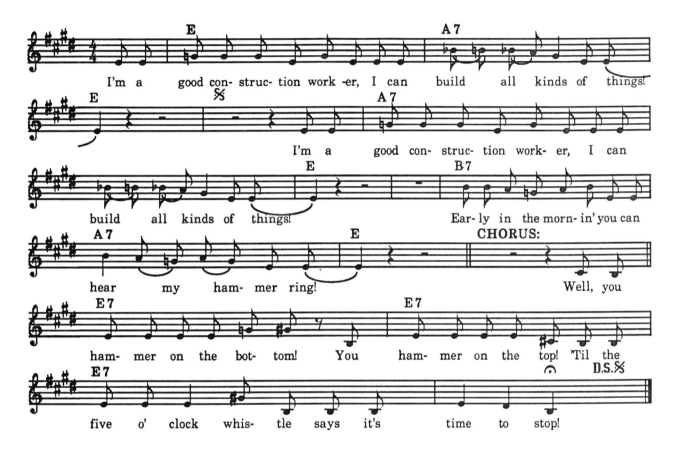

2. I'm workin' on a building, ninety-nine stories high!
   I'm workin' on a building, ninety-nine stories high!
   I make my livin' way up in the sky!

   (CHORUS)

3. I'm walkin' on a girder, watchin' the world below!
   I'm walkin' on a girder, watchin' the world below!
   I'm a good construction worker, gonna make this buildin' grow!

   (CHORUS)

Title: Helicopter

Skills: creates dramatic scenes at flannelboard
acts out a dramatic sequence
discovers a nature-made toy

Development: **Materials:**

A. Awakening . . .

> Provide a flannelboard with the following felt pieces: airplane,   flannelboard
> jet, glider, helicopter, airport hangar and tower, clouds, etc. (see   felt pieces
> Appendix pg. 229). Encourage the children to learn the names of   shoebox
> the various "flying machines" by manipulating the pieces and
> creating their own aviation adventures.
>
> Ask the children to store the felt pieces in a labeled shoebox
> for future use.

B. Celebrating . . .

> Invite the children to take turns acting out the sequence of events   control tower
> in the song, using their whole body to twirl like a helicopter.   props
> Provide a large space for them to move in, as they spread out their
> arms like helicopter blades.
>
> Suggest that the rest of the children pretend to be working
> in the control tower. Let them invent their own props, such as
> blocks for radios, paper plates for radar screens, etc.

C. Embracing . . .

> Take a field walk and look for maple leaf "helicopters." Show the   maple leaves
> children how to spin the leaves through the air!
>
> Ask the children to notice what is similar between a maple
> leaf "helicopter" and a real helicopter (the leaves are shaped like
> propellors).

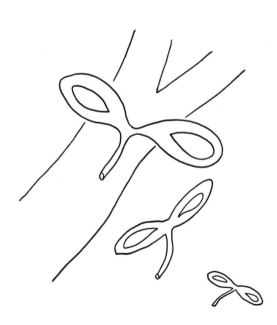

(bouncy)

words and music:
Bob Messano

Helicopter

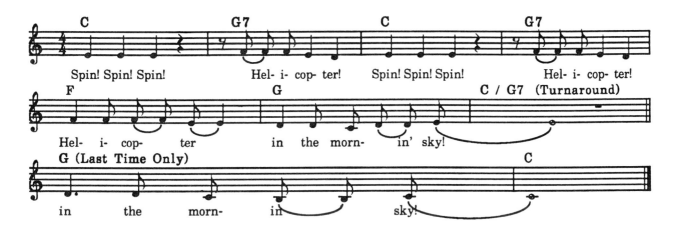

Spin! Spin! Spin!   Hel- i- cop- ter!   Spin! Spin! Spin!   Hel- i- cop- ter!

Hel- i- cop- ter   in the morn- in' sky!

in the morn- in' sky!

2. Rum! Rum! Rum! Hear the engine!
   Rum! Rum! Rum! Hear the engine!
   Helicopter in the mornin' sky!

3. Zip! Zip! Zip! Big propellor!
   Zip! Zip! Zip! Big propellor!
   Helicopter in the mornin' sky!

4. Bump! Bump! Bump! It's gettin' windy!
   Bump! Bump! Bump! It's gettin' windy!
   Helicopter in the mornin' sky!

5. Out of gas! Make a landing!
   Out of gas! Make a landing!
   Helicopter in the mornin' sky!

6. Fill 'er up! Start the engine!
   Fill 'er up! Start the engine!
   Helicopter in the mornin' sky!

(repeat first verse)

Title: **I Don't Wanna Be Extinct**

Skills: responds to poetry
interprets song through puppetry
identifies dinosaurs

Development: **Materials:**

A. Awakening . . .

Introduce the song with the following poem: words to poem

> Scrunchasaurus,
> Munchasaurus,
> Crunchasaurus, too.
> If you run out of dinosaurs,
> Just make up something new . . .
>
> Rumblesaurus,
> Mumblesaurus,
> Grumblesaurus Rex.
> All of them with tiny brains,
> Upon their mighty necks!

Ask the children to make up their own silly names for dinosaurs.

B. Celebrating . . .

Sing the song and invite the children to join in singing the   paper bags
CHORUS. Help them to gradually learn the rest of the words   markers
through repeated singing.   buttons
    Let the children make paper bag puppets to use for the   yarn
dinosaur's speaking part in the song. Provide paper bags, mark-   glue
ers, buttons, glue, and other art materials for their creative   assorted art
representations of dinosaurs.   materials

C. Embracing . . .

Invite the children to join in a "Dinosaur Hunt." Ask another   plastic
teacher or aide to take everyone outside while you hide plastic   dinosaurs
dinosaur figures around the classroom.
    Challenge the children to locate the dinosaurs when they
return. Help them to name their discoveries by matching them up
with pictures of dinosaurs in books or on posters.

(with Spirit)

words and music:
Bob Messano

I Don't Wanna Be Extinct!

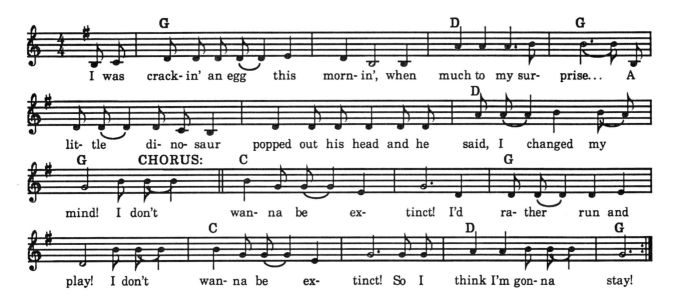

I was crack-in' an egg this morn-in', when much to my sur-prise... A lit-tle di-no-saur popped out his head and he said, I changed my mind! **CHORUS:** I don't wan-na be ex-tinct! I'd ra-ther run and play! I don't wan-na be ex-tinct! So I think I'm gon-na stay!

2. I went to tell my mother, about this dinosaur,
   And we could hear him singin' as he headed out that door!

   (CHORUS)

3. I took the dinosaur to school, he scared the teachers away,
   But all the children weren't afraid of the games he liked to play!

   (CHORUS)

4. Now he's very happy, he sleeps right by my bed,
   And if you ever see him, just remember what he said!

   (CHORUS)

129

Title: **I'm a Little Birdy**

Skills: enjoys field trips
plays a dramatic role
observes and identifies birds

Development: **Materials:**

A. Awakening . . .

Visit a pet store and observe the colorful variety of birds. Arrange   birdfeeder
for an employee to give the children a short talk about the bird's   birdseed
names, habits, eating preferences, etc.
Encourage the children to make comments and ask questions about the birds.
Purchase a birdfeeder and birdseed from the store.

B. Celebrating . . .

Play a dramatic musical game, as follows: two blankets
Spread out two different color blankets on the ground out-
side. Give the children a choice of which blanket they would like
to sit on. Ask them to pretend that the blankets are their nests
and that they are birds.
Invite the children to take turns flying away from their
nests when they hear the words: *"I'm flying!"* and to return when
they hear the words: *"I always come back to the tree!"*
Ask them what kinds of things they saw on their flight.

C. Embracing . . .

Set up a birdfeeder outside the classroom window. Show the   birdfeeder
children pictures of commonly seen birds in your area. If possible,   birdseed
cut out the pictures and mount them on large index cards. Play a   pictures of birds
flashcard guessing game to help the children learn the names of   index cards
the birds.   paste
Encourage the children to share in the responsibility for
refilling the birdfeeder.

130

words and music:
Bob Messano

I'm a Little Birdy

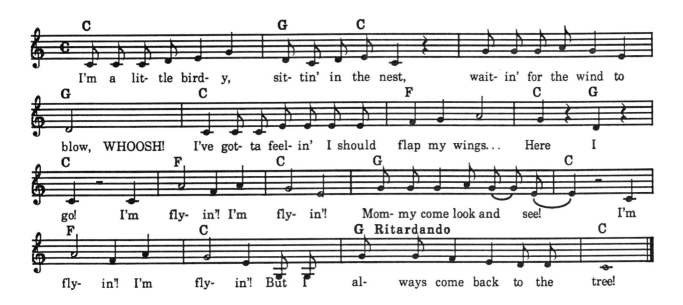

I'm a lit- tle bird- y, sit- tin' in the nest, wait- in' for the wind to blow, WHOOSH! I've got- ta feel- in' I should flap my wings... Here I go! I'm fly- in'! I'm fly- in'! Mom- my come look and see! I'm fly- in'! I'm fly- in'! But I al- ways come back to the tree!

Variations:

I'm a little blue jay . . .

I'm a little robin . . .

I'm a little nuthatch . . .

I'm a little goldfinch . . .

(etc.)

Title: **I've Got a Big Plane**

Skills: shows curiosity

plays a dramatic role, using props

records observations of field trip

Development:	Materials:

A. Awakening . . .

Set up an interest center about airplanes and aviation. Place materials, such as the following, on or near a table: model airplanes, paper airplanes, picture books, posters, an airplane mobile, etc.

Encourage the children to explore the materials with your guidance. Respond to their questions and comments with informative answers and leading questions. For example:

What kind of plane can fly without a motor? (a glider)

aviation materials

B. Celebrating . . .

Invite some of the children to act out the song sequence by pretending to be airplanes. Ask the other children to play the part of the ground crew who service the planes. Provide them with props such as plastic tools, empty squirt-bottles for "fuel," plastic goggles, etc.

For variation, try the song in the "wild blue yonder" outdoors. Designate a hangar, such as the area underneath a playground climber, where the planes can be readied for flight.

ground crew props

C. Embracing . . .

Visit a local airport! Arrange for a member of the airport staff to provide a simple introduction to the workings of the airport and/ or planes.

Hold a "Sky Watch" where the children make pictures of things they see go by in the sky. Display the drawings in the classroom and ask the children to describe their favorite part of the trip.

crayons

paper

words and music:
Bob Messano

I've Got a Big Plane

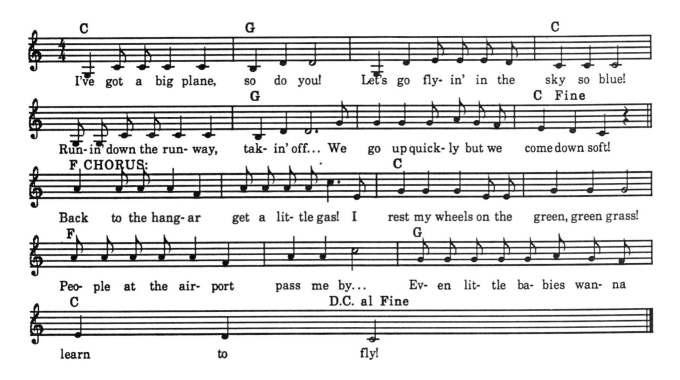

I've got a big plane, so do you! Let's go fly- in' in the sky so blue!

Run- in' down the run- way, tak- in' off... We go up quick- ly but we come down soft!

CHORUS: Back to the hang- ar get a lit- tle gas! I rest my wheels on the green, green grass!

Peo- ple at the air- port pass me by... Ev- en lit- tle ba- bies wan- na

learn to fly!

Variations:

I've got a jet plane . . .

I've got a biplane . . .

I've got a seaplane . . .

(etc.)

Title: **It Looks Like a Unicorn**

Skills: responds to poetry
plays a dramatic role; plays melody bells
enjoys growing things

Development: **Materials:**

A. Awakening . . .

Share the following poem: words to poem

> *Long, long ago,*
> *In a land beyond the sea,*
> *I met a beautiful creature,*
> *She turned to look at me!*
> *With a body like a pony,*
> *And a gleaming silver horn,*
> *She said these words and left me . . .*
> *My name is Unicorn!*

Ask the children why they think the unicorn was shy.

B. Celebrating . . .

Play a dramatic musical game, as follows: melody bells
Invite some of the children to pretend to be unicorns. Ask
the rest of the children to ring melody bells as the unicorns
prance. Trade places and repeat.
For variation, perform the song outdoors. Ask the children
who are playing bells to form a circle. Challenge the unicorns to
weave in and out of the circle.

C. Embracing . . .

Create a "Unicorn Garden!" An old aquarium can be transformed   aquarium
into a planter for easy-to-grow vegetables such as peas, radishes,   soil
or carrots. Encourage the children to share the responsibility for   vegetable seeds
watering and caring for the garden.
Be available to respond to the children's daily observations,
exclamations, and questions as the plants develop.

(dramatically)

words and music:
Bob Messano

It Looks Like a Unicorn

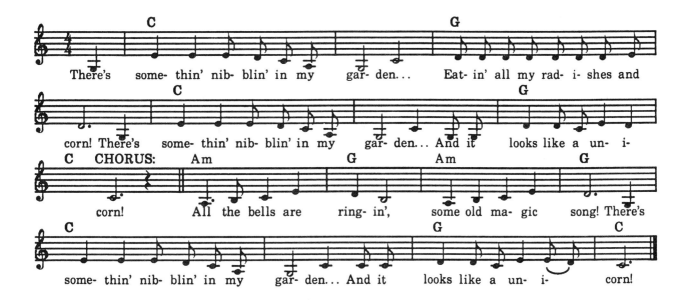

There's some- thin' nib- blin' in my gar- den... Eat- in' all my rad- i- shes and corn! There's some- thin' nib- blin' in my gar- den... And it looks like a un- i- corn!

CHORUS: All the bells are ring- in', some old ma- gic song! There's some- thin' nib- blin' in my gar- den... And it looks like a un- i- corn!

2. There's somethin' dancin' in my garden . . .
I can see the glimmer of a horn!
There's somethin' dancin' in my garden . . .
And it looks like a unicorn!

(CHORUS)

3. There's somethin' sleepin' in my garden . . .
I can see it early in the morn!
There's somethin' sleepin' in my garden . . .
And it looks like a unicorn!

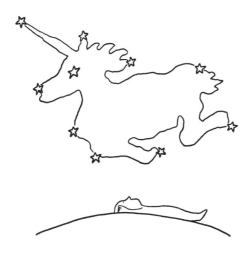

135

Title: Little Flower

Skills: enjoys field trips
uses descriptive language
observes and records growth process of plants

Development: **Materials:**

A. Awakening . . .

Visit a garden supply shop! Arrange for an employee to show the   flower seedlings
children the various kinds of tools, soil, and seeds that a gardener
uses. Encourage them to make comments and ask questions.

Purchase some marigold seedlings or other easy-to-grow
flowers for the children to re-plant.

Talk about the trip in the classroom, encouraging the children to recall growing experiences they have had at home and
school.

B. Celebrating . . .

Play a musical game, as follows: paper plates

Give each child a paper plate and some crayons. Ask them to   crayons
draw a flower face on their plate.
                                                                         pom-poms
As the children hold the plates in their lap, walk around the
room singing the song and make it rain by dropping colorful pom-
poms (available in craft stores) on their plates.

Encourage the children to talk about their thirsty flowers!

C. Embracing . . .

Let the children re-plant flower seedlings! Provide soil, shovels,   seedlings
and a watering can. Guide the children through the steps of re-   soil
planting, emphasizing gentle handling of the seedlings. Create a   shovels
school garden or window box!   watering can

Encourage the children to watch their plants closely over time.   paper
Ask them to draw pictures of their plants at various stages, such   crayons
as: forming buds, producing flowers, attracting bees, etc. Compile   stapler
the pictures into a book called "Our Flower Story" with the
children's names and comments included.

136

(tenderly)

words and music:
Bob Messano

Little Flower

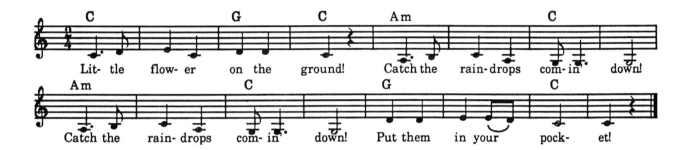

Lit- tle   flow- er   on the   ground!   Catch the   rain- drops   com- in'   down!

Catch the   rain- drops   com- in'   down!   Put them   in your   pock-   et!

2. Little flower in the wood!
   Feel the sunshine, it's so good!
   Feel the sunshine, it's so good!
   Good to warm your pockets!

3. Little flower in the shade!
   Toss your head and gently sway!
   Toss your head and gently sway!
   The wind will fill your pockets!

4. Little flower, grow so high!
   Stand up tall and touch the sky!
   Stand up tall and touch the sky!
   Laughter in your pockets!

Title: **The Mud Song**

Skills: responds to puppetry
acts out a musical sequence
explores the nature of mud

Development:

Materials:

A. Awakening . . .

Make a "Chef Piggy" hand puppet (see Appendix pg. 230). Have the puppet ask the children to help him make a special mud pie. List the ingredients suggested by the children.

Encourage the children to pantomime the steps in making a mud pie, as follows: scooping up some dirt, pouring in some water, making a mud ball, flattening and patting it into a mud pie.

puppet pattern
paper bag
markers
scissors
glue

B. Celebrating . . .

Invite the children to act out the musical sequence by moving their bodies. Ask them to begin by pretending to hold a bucket of water in their hands. Encourage everyone to make the sound of water being poured on the ground and to use their whole body as they squish the mud.

Adapt the song for a small group of children by putting the children's names into the song. For example:

Well, (Child's name)'s got a bucketful a'water . . .

C. Embracing . . .

Give the children the opportunity to experiment with mud-making. Provide a plastic basin filled with soil, plastic shovels, cups and pails, and a watering can. Make sure that the children wear smocks to protect their clothing.

Ask each child to fill a plastic cup with their own mud mixture. Place the cups on a sunny windowsill. Encourage the children to guess what will happen to the mud if it is left there awhile. Ask them to check their mud cup by feeling it with their finger every once in a while.

basin
soil
shovels
cups
pails
watering can
smocks

words and music:
Bob Messano

The Mud Song

We'll I've got a buck-et full of wa-ter! I'm gon-na pour it on the ground! I'm gon-na make a whole lot-ta good ol' mud and squish my toes all a- round!

2. Well, you've got a bucket full of water!
You're gonna pour it on the ground!
You're gonna make a whole lotta good ol' mud . . .
And squish your toes all around!

3. Well, we've got a bucket full of water!
We're gonna pour it on the ground!
We're gonna make a whole lotta good ol' mud . . .
And then we're gonna sit right down!

Title: **Put Your Ear to a Seashell**

Skills: enjoys tactile explorations
accompanies song with hand motions; uses props
explores the formation of fossils

Development: **Materials:**

A. Awakening . . .

Bury a variety of seashells in a sand table or other basin filled   seashells
with sand. Challenge the children to discover the "buried trea-   sand table
sure" by digging in the sand.
    Encourage the children to take turns playing this same
hide-and-seek game with their classmates. Leave the seashells in
the sand table for the children to use in their pretend play. They
will invent many uses for them!

B. Celebrating . . .

Suggest that the children accompany the song with hand motions   crepe paper
and sound-effects, such as the following:

> *Put your ear to a seashell!*
> (cup hand around ear)
> *And you can hear the sea!*
> (make wavy motions and sounds)

For variation, invite the children to wave blue and green crepe
paper streamers to represent the motion of the sea!

C. Embracing . . .

Let the children make "fossils" of seashells. Invite them to help   seashells
mix up some craft plaster. Pour the plaster into plastic plates and   craft plaster
encourage the children to make imprints of seashells. Allow the   plastic plates
plaster to harden.   natural objects
    Encourage the children to experiment with this process,
using rocks, leaves, ferns, bones, feathers, and other objects found
in nature. Create a classroom "Fossil Museum" with the results!

words and music:
Bob Messano

Put Your Ear to a Seashell

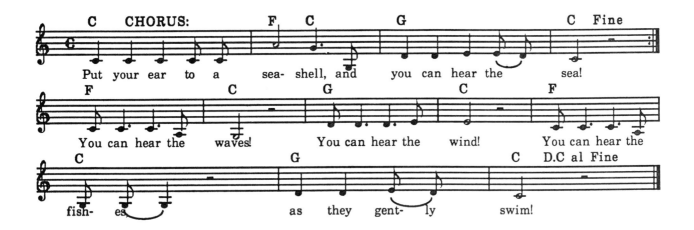

Put your ear to a sea-shell, and you can hear the sea!
You can hear the waves! You can hear the wind! You can hear the
fish- es as they gent- ly swim!

(CHORUS)

2. You you hear the gulls! You can hear the sails!
   You can hear the dolphins talking to the whales!

(CHORUS)

3. You can hear the roar! You can hear the crash!
   You can hear the children making such a splash!

(CHORUS)

Title: **The Rainbow Sea**

Skills: names sea creatures
plays a cooperative game
explores the formation of waves on water

Development: **Materials:**

A. Awakening . . .

Introduce the song with the following story: words to story

*Once there was a ship that carried barrels of colors across the sea.
One day, a great storm shook the ship and the barrels rolled
overboard. All the colors spilled out and swirled in the water. That
is why there are so many colorful creatures in the sea today!*

Ask the children to name some sea creatures.

B. Celebrating . . .

Invite the children to play a cooperative parachute game! Choose   parachute
some of the children to be the wave-makers while the others are
the swimmers.
   Encourage the wave-makers to hold onto the edges of the
recreational-parachute; and to make waves by moving their arms
rapidly up and down. Invite the swimmers to go under the parachute and to make swimming motions as they sing the song.
Trade places and repeat.

C. Embracing . . .

Set up a wave-making experiment! Place a large aluminum foil   foil pan
roasting pan on a table. Fill one-third of the pan with water and   water
add food coloring.   food coloring
   Place a drum and drum stick on the table. Encourage the   drum
children to take turns beating the drum and making waves. Ask   drum stick
the children what they think made the waves.

words and music:
Bob Messano

The Rainbow Sea

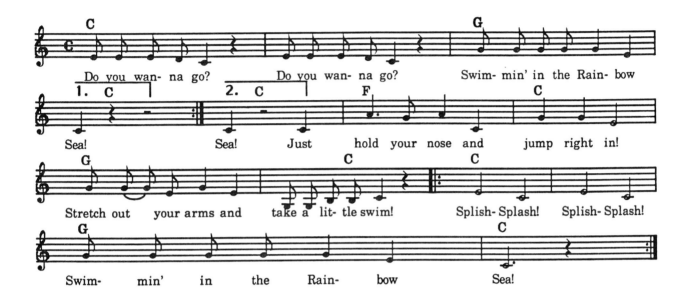

Do you wan- na go? Do you wan- na go? Swim- min' in the Rain- bow

Sea! Sea! Just hold your nose and jump right in!

Stretch out your arms and take a lit- tle swim! Splish- Splash! Splish- Splash!

Swim- min' in the Rain- bow Sea!

Variation:

(Child's name)'s gonna go . . .

Title: The Snow

Skills: reads symbols

performs a sequence of hand motions

describes weather conditions using puppetry

Development: **Materials:**

A. Awakening . . .

Make a rebus chart with the words to the song (see Appendix pg.   oak tag
231). Substitute pictures for the following words: *snow, moun-*   markers
tains, trees, ocean, me. Encourage the children to read along as
you point to the words and pictures.

Place the chart in the "Science/Discovery Area" of the classroom for the children to read independently, to themselves or to
their friends.

B. Celebrating . . .

Invite the children to make hand motions to the song, such as the   none
following:

The snow is falling on the mountains!
(bring down snow with hands; make a mountain peak with two hands)
The snow is falling on the trees!
(bring down snow with hands; spread arms up and out like branches)
The snow is falling on the ocean!
(bring down snow with hands; make wave motions with arms)
The snow is falling on me!
(bring down snow with hands; point to self)

C. Embracing . . .

Let the children use a set of hand puppets which animate the   paper bags
weather (see Appendix pg. 232)! Invite them to take turns being   markers
the "Class Weather Reporters," selecting a puppet to describe the   storage box
weather outside.

Place the puppets in a labeled box in the "Science/Discovery
Area" of the classroom for the children to use independently.

words and music:
Bob Messano

(gently)

The Snow

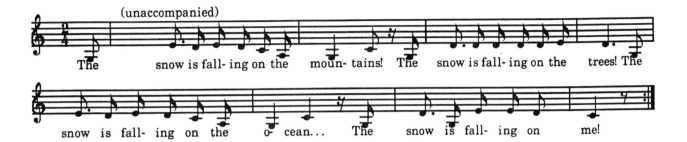

(unaccompanied)

The snow is fall-ing on the moun-tains! The snow is fall-ing on the trees! The snow is fall-ing on the o-cean... The snow is fall-ing on me!

2. It's chilly, chilly on the mountains . . .

3. It's blowing, blowing on the mountains . . .

4. It's melting, melting on the mountains . . .

145

Title: **Time to Listen**

Skills: responds to poetry
imitates animal sounds; adapts song lyrics
explores an animals' adaptation to its environment

Development: **Materials:**

A. Awakening . . .

Share the following poem: words to poem

> *if you listen to goose music*
> *you may hear the voices*
> *of cold faraway places*
> *where the reeds rustle*
> *the hatching of goose eggs*
> *while the winds whistle*
> *the lifting of wings*
> *in the sky castle*
> *do you listen to goose music?*
> *what does it say to you?*

B. Celebrating . . .

Invite the children to make sounds of geese in the song.   none
Encourage the children to adapt the song by putting in the
names of other birds and their sounds. For example:

> *It's time to listen and look at the sky!*
> *A flock of (crows) is flyin' by!*
> *And the first one says, ("Caw!")*
> *And the second one says, ("Caw! Caw!")*
> *And the third one says, "WAIT FOR ME!"*

C. Embracing . . .

Show the children a goose feather and place a drop of water on it   goose feathers
with a plastic eye dropper. Challenge the children to pass the   eye droppers
feather from person to person, trying not to drop the drop!
Ask the children why they think the water makes a bead on   cups of water
the feather instead of soaking in.
Place some feathers, cups of water, and eye droppers in the
"Science/Discovery Area" for the children to explore independently.

146

(dramatically)

words and music:
Bob Messano

Time to Listen

It's time to list- en and look at the sky! A flock of geese is fly- in' by! And the first one says, "HONK!" And the sec- ond one says, "HONK! HONK!" And the third one says, "WAIT FOR ME!"

2. The geese have landed on the lake!
   Listen to the sounds they make!

   (CHORUS)

3. The gray of winter's in the sky!
   Very soon the geese will fly!

   (CHORUS)

4. Now the geese have said goodbye!
   We can hear them flying high!

   (CHORUS)

147

Title: **The Tree's Song**

Skills: reads symbols

performs a sequence of body movements

explores a mini-environment

Development: **Materials:**

A. Awakening . . .

Create a "Music Tree" for the classroom (see pg. 233). Make ornaments for the tree representing the children's favorite songs. For example, a small bundle of sticks could represent *The Trees' Song!*

Let the children take turns choosing their favorite songs to sing and act out during "Circle Time" each day. Add new sets of ornaments corresponding to new songs.

Materials: coffee can, tree branch, pebbles

B. Celebrating . . .

Invite the children to perform a sequence of body movements to accompany the song, as follows:

Materials: rhythm sticks

CHORUS: slap thighs with hands in rhythm

Verse 1:   bend to ground; cup hands, pretend to drink water

Verse 2:   reach arms in the air like branches; sway body/wave arms

Verse 3:   reach arms to the side; touch someone gently

For variation, encourage some children to tap the beat with rhythm sticks while the others pretend to be trees. Trade places and repeat.

C. Embracing . . .

Visit a tree in the park, playground or neighborhood. Make a large, rough circle around the tree by laying out a long piece of yarn. Ask the children to stay within the circle as they search for interesting things.

Provide a collection box where the children's discoveries can be accumulated. Bring the box to the classroom and place it in the "Science/Discovery Area" for the children to explore further.

Materials: yarn, box

words and music:
Bob Messano

The Tree's Song

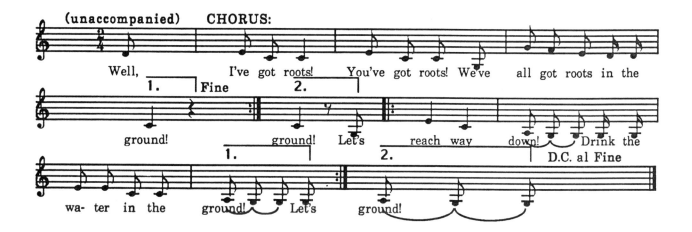

(unaccompanied)   CHORUS:

Well, I've got roots! You've got roots! We've all got roots in the ground!

1. Fine   2. ground! Let's reach way down! Drink the

1.   2.   D.C. al Fine

wa- ter in the ground! Let's ground!

2. Let's reach up high! Wave our branches in the sky!
   Let's reach up high! Wave our branches in the sky!

   (CHORUS)

3. Let's reach to the side! Spread our branches wide!
   Let's reach to the side! Spread our branches wide!

   (CHORUS)

Title: **Up in the Pine Cone Tree**

Skills: collects the bounty of nature
plays a dramatic role
creates a bird feeder from natural materials

Development:	**Materials:**

A. Awakening . . .

Take a field walk to gather pine cones. If you do not have a pine tree nearby, collect the cones yourself or ask a friend to gather some for you. Hide the pine cones in the classroom and let the children search for them!

pine cones

Encourage the children to smell the pine cones and feel them. Place some in the "Science/Discovery Area" for the children to explore further.

B. Celebrating . . .

Invite a small group of children to take turns playing the part of the bird in the song. Ask each child to stand on a sturdy milk crate, representing their tree. Encourage the rest of the children to sing, clap, or whistle along to the song.

milk crate

Ask each bird to pick someone to take their place after the song has been sung.

C. Embracing . . .

Let the children make pine cone bird feeders! Cover a table with a washable tablecloth. Give each child a pine cone with a pipe cleaner tied on the top (suitable for hanging) and a plastic knife. Provide a tub of peanut butter for the children to use in filling in the spaces on the pine cone.

tablecloth
pine cones
pipe cleaners
peanut butter
plastic knife
bowl
birdseed

Guide the children in rolling their sticky pine cones in a bowl of birdseed. Hang the feeders in branches outside.

(jubilantly)

**words and music:
Bob Messano**

Up in the Pine Cone Tree

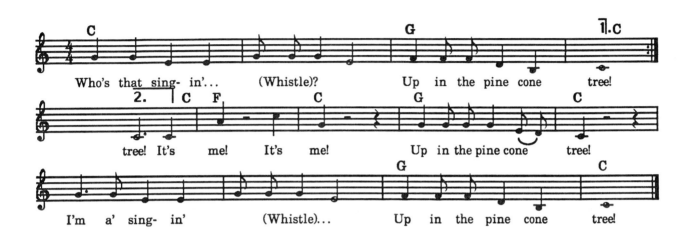

Who's that sing- in'... (Whistle)? Up in the pine cone tree!

tree! It's me! It's me! Up in the pine cone tree!

I'm a' sing- in' (Whistle)... Up in the pine cone tree!

Title: **We're in a Spaceship**

Skills: shows curiosity

performs a series of body movements

plays imaginatively

Development:	**Materials:**

A. Awakening . . .

Set up a "Space Station." Place objects related to space travel and exploration on and around a table. For example: models of spacecraft, astronaut figures, posters, mobile of planets, space picture books, etc.

Encourage the children to investigate the materials. Respond to their comments, insights and questions.

space-related objects

B. Celebrating . . .

Make a picture of a spaceship with four control buttons (see Appendix, pg. 234). Show the children the picture as you sing the song. Press the buttons and announce the following spaceship commands.

oak tag

markers

red button: everybody move fast
green button: everybody move in a silly way
yellow button: everybody move very slowly
brown button: everybody hop up and down

Vary the tempo of the song according to the commands!

C. Embracing . . .

Create a spaceship from a large appliance box. Invite the children to take turns playing inside. Set a time limit so that everyone has a fair chance to play (use an egg timer with bell).

Invite the children to become astronauts. Challenge them to accomplish various missions, such as the following:

appliance box

paint

paintbrushes

egg timer

Gather food for the space flight!
Gas up the spaceship!
Walk in space!

152

words and music:
Bob Messano

(playfully)

We're in a Spaceship

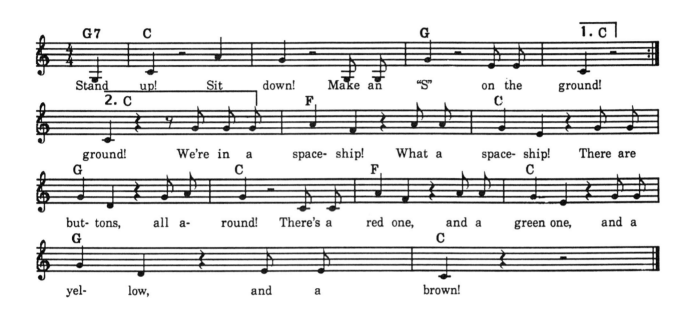

Stand up! Sit down! Make an "S" on the ground! ground! We're in a space-ship! What a space-ship! There are but-tons, all a-round! There's a red one, and a green one, and a yel-low, and a brown!

Title: **Why Do the River Go Up?**

Skills: listens with interest
plays rhythm instruments; dances to music
experiments with bubbles; adapts song lyrics

Development:	**Materials:**

A. Awakening . . .

Introduce the song with the following story: words to story

Once there was a silly river where all kinds of crazy things happened. You might see a fish paddling a canoe! You might see a turtle with heads on both ends! You might see a family of ducks eating peanut butter sandwiches!
One night, under a full moon, all the animals started to sing a silly tune . . .

B. Celebrating . . .

Invite some of the children to give the song a calypso beat by   rhythm
playing Caribbean rhythm instruments, such as the following: instruments
guiro, maraccas, steel drums or xylophones, castanets, etc.
Ask the rest of the children to dance and act out the song
using body movements and gestures. Trade places and repeat.

C. Embracing . . .

Let the children explore bubble-making and bubble-blowing. Mix   liquid soap
liquid soap and water and provide bubble-blowers. Encourage   water
them to adapt the song, as in the following example: paper cups
   bubble-blowers

Why do the (bubbles) go up?
Why do the (bubbles) go down?
I don't know why the (bubbles) go up,
but when I sneeze (ACHOO!) . . .
The (bubbles) go down!

(calypso)

**words and music:
Bob Messano**

Why Do the River Go Up?

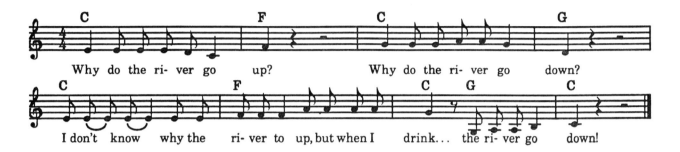

Why do the ri- ver go up? Why do the ri- ver go down?

I don't know why the ri- ver to up, but when I drink... the ri- ver go down!

2. Why do the sun go up?
   Why do the sun go down?
   I don't know why the sun go up . . .
   But when I blink, the sun go down!

3. Why do the moon go up?
   Why do the moon go down?
   I don't know why the moon go up . . .
   But when I wink, the moon go down!

Section 4

A Sense of Friendship (Music-social studies activities)

This section integrates music and social studies. The songs and activities are particularly suitable for promoting children's compatibility with others and the environment. Children are encouraged to grow in caring and cooperative attitudes for successful living.

Bald Eagle	*learning a national symbol*
Best, Best Friend	*socializing with other children*
Broken Bears	*imaginative play*
Bye, Bye Butterfly	*taking turns speaking*
The City Squirrel	*relating experiences*
Come In	*participates in a celebration*
Diggin' in the Mine	*using descriptive language*
He Sowed a Seed	*celebrating Martin Luther King*
If I Was an Apple . . .	*supermarket field trip*
I Like You Very Much	*sharing music with parents*
I'm Jumpin'	*cooperative game play*
Johnny Appleseed	*participates in a celebration*
Let's Make a Pancake	*pizza parlor field trip*
Let's Play Our Guitars	*communicating with a guest*
Native American Song	*exploring different lifestyles*
A New Thanksgiving Song	*expressing thanks to others*
Panda Played Piano	*experimenting with music-making*
A Quiet Place	*enjoying quiet activities*
Sam the Clam's Blues	*participates in a celebration*
The Water and the Old Mill Wheel	*sharing with others*
We Make Music	*teaching others*
We're Goin' Skatin'	*participates in a celebration*
We Wiggle When We Wash Our Hands	*self-care (hygiene)*
Who Is Friends with a Cat?	*making classroom rules*
Will You Be My Cuddly Panda Bear?	*sharing music with parents*

Title: Bald Eagle

Skills: responds to puppetry and poetry
acts out a song using body movements; follows directions
becomes familiar with a national symbol

Development: **Materials:**

A. Awakening . . .

Make a "Bald Eagle" hand puppet (see Appendix, pg. 235). Have   puppet pattern
the puppet share the following poem: lunch bag
                                                                    markers
                                                                    scissors
                                                                    glue

> *I am a Bald Eagle,*
> *These are my wings!*
> *Up to my nest,*
> *I bring squirming things!*
>
> *Fish from the rivers,*
> *Mice from the ground,*
> *I watch from the sky . . .*
> *And then I swoop down!*

Make the puppet swoop down at the end of the poem. Let the
children pretend to feed it. Ask each child what they are giving to
the eagle.

B. Celebrating . . .

Invite the children to act out the song by pretending to fly like a   none
bald eagle. After they have become familiar with the song, encourage them to originate their own answers to the questions
posed by the lyrics. Let them interpret their answers through
creative movement.
   Adapt the song for an outdoor game by inserting directions
into the lyrics which the group can perform. For example:

> *We'll go to the tree and circle around!*
> *Circle around! Circle around!*
> *We'll go to the tree and circle around . . .*
> *In the land of America!*
> *In the land of America!*

C. Embracing . . .

Show the children the pictures of bald eagles on the U.S. one-   one-dollar bill
dollar bill and quarter. Let the children handle the money.   quarter
   Encourage the children to notice other representations of
the bald eagle throughout the community (at the post office,
library, civic buildings, recruiting stations, atop flap poles, etc.).

(flowing)

words and music:
Bob Messano

Bald Eagle

Oh, Bald Ea- gle, where did you go? Where did you go? Where did you go?

Oh, Bald Ea- gle, where did you go? Why did you fly a- way?

2. I went to the river to look for some fish!
Look for some fish! Look for some fish!
I went to the river to look for some fish . . .
In the land of America!
In the land of America!

(CHORUS)

3. I went to the mountain to raise my young!
Raise my young! Raise my young!
I went to the mountain to raise my young . . .
In the land of America!
In the land of America!

(CHORUS)

4. I went to the forest to find a home!
Find a home! Find a home!
I went to the forest to find a home . . .
In the land of America!
In the land of America!

(CHORUS)

159

Title: **Best, Best Friend**

Skills: responds to poetry
plays a dramatic role
socializes/plays with other children

Development: **Materials:**

A. Awakening . . .

Share the following poem: words to poem

> *My best, best friend is very quiet,*
> *But if there's a game he'll always try it.*
> *Wherever I go, he follows near,*
> *But on cloudy days he disappears.*
> *Perhaps he's hiding 'round the bend . . .*
> *My shadow is my best, best friend!*

Ask the children what kinds of things they like to do with their
friends.

B. Celebrating . . .

Invite the children to play a dramatic musical game, as follows: none
Choose one child to play the part of the "friend in the house,"
while another plays the part of the "friend who comes to play."
Ask the first child to pick a place in the classroom to be their
"house."
Encourage the children to act out the lyrics as you sing the
first verse of the song. Give everyone a turn to play!

C. Embracing . . .

Arrange a special "Visiting Time" when the children can meet   up to you
and play with children of different ages in other classes in the
school. Provide a common ground for new friendships by arrang-
ing some cooperative activities, such as the following:

> *play a group game*
>
> *share a homemade snack*
>
> *share a special song*
>
> *make a mural*

(cheerfully)

words and music:
Bob Messano

Best, Best Friend

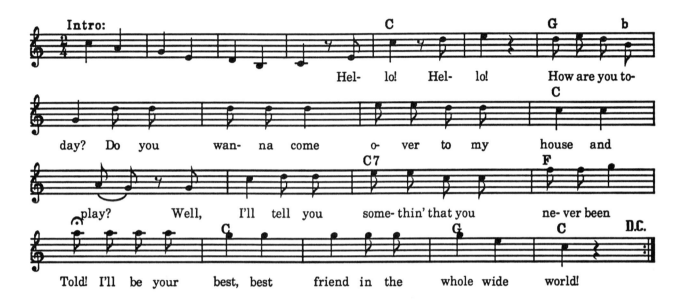

Intro:

C   G   b

Hel- lo! Hel- lo!   How are you to-

C

day? Do you wan- na come   o- ver to my   house and

C7   F

play? Well, I'll tell you   some- thin' that you   ne- ver been

C   G   C   D.C.

Told! I'll be your   best, best   friend in the   whole wide   world!

2. We could throw rocks in the ol' frog pond!
   We could make magic with my magic wand!
   There's a very special toy that I'll let you hold . . .
   I'll be your best, best friend in the whole wide world!

3. We could have a picnic by the apple tree!
   I could share with you and you could share with me!
   We'll always be together 'till we're ninety-years-old . . .
   I'll be your best, best friend in the whole wide world!

   (repeat first verse)

Title: Broken Bears

Skills: discusses feelings
plays a dramatic role
plays imaginatively

Development: **Materials:**

A. Awakening . . .

Give each child a picture of a "Broken Bear" (see Appendix, pg. 236). Ask them how they think the bear is feeling. What could have happened to it?

Provide each child with a few small adhesive bandages, and ask them to "repair their bears." Assist younger children in manipulating the bandages. Ask them how they think the bear is feeling after being cared for. Encourage everyone to describe the times they have had bumps, cuts, bruises, etc.

copies of bear picture
adhesive bandages

B. Celebrating . . .

Invite the children to play a dramatic musical game, as follows:

Show the children a hospital sign (see Appendix, pg. 237) Designate one area of the classroom "the hospital" by placing the sign there.

Ask some of the children to play the parts of "Broken Bears" while the rest of the children pretend to be "Doctors." Encourage the bears to walk around, acting hurt, and for the doctors to bring the bears to the hospital for repairs. Trade places and repeat.

oak tag
markers
doctor props

C. Embracing . . .

Make a "Hospital Prop Box" available for the children's use. Include such items as the following: play stethoscope, medical bag, sling, blanket, bandages, etc. Encourage the children to act out the roles of doctors and patients.

For variation, invite the children to bring in stuffed animals from home to be their patients. Encourage them to talk about their own experiences in doctor's offices and hospitals.

hospital props
prop box

(lovingly)

words and music:
Bob Messano

Broken Bears

Bro- ken Bears with rips and tears, and all the fluff gone out!
I know a per- son who does re- pairs, we'll try and fig- ure it out! You
walk a- bout in a flop- py way, noth- in' to hold you in! We'll take you by your
fur- ry hand and fix you up a- gain!

2. Here come the bears on hands and knees,
   Crawling as best as they can!
   It isn't easy when you are old,
   And always in need of a hand!

   (CHORUS)

3. Now, all the bears are sewn up tight,
   The magic is back in their eyes!
   And as the children fall to sleep,
   They grow to a fabulous size!

   (CHORUS)

   (repeat first verse and CHORUS)

Title: Bye, Bye, Butterfly

Skills: performs creative movements to poetry
moves gently
appreciates what others have to say

Development:	**Materials:**

A. Awakening . . .

Share the following dramatic poem and encourage the children to act out the sequence:

words to poem

> *Caterpillars cuddle,*
> *Beneath the autumn moon,*
> *All wrapped up in silver threads,*
> *Snug in their cocoons*
>
> *And when the winter's over,*
> *To everyone's surprise,*
> *They open up their tiny doors . . .*
> *And out come butterflies!*

B. Celebrating . . .

Invite the children to act out the song by making the gentle motions of butterfly wings by moving their arms. Provide a large open space for them to perform the song.

none

For variation, use the song as a transition-time activity. Give the children a group direction, such as:

> *Let's fly like butterflies to the snack table!*

C. Embracing . . .

Schedule a "Going Home Time" each day. Gather the children in a comfortable place to talk about the day's activities, share a few words about the art they have created, sing favorite songs, etc.

puppet pattern
wooden craft stick
scissors
crayons
glue

One technique to help the children focus on one speaker at a time involves a butterfly stick puppet (see Appendix, pg. 238). Ask them to take turns holding the puppet and speaking, and passing on the puppet when they are ready to give another person a turn to speak.

(gently)

**words: Bob Messano
music: adapted "Skip To My Lou"**

Bye, Bye, Butterfly

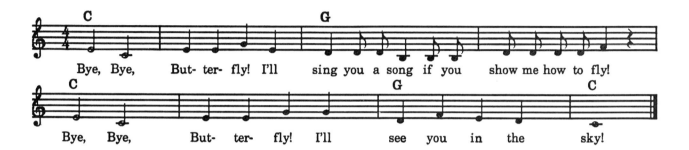

Bye, Bye, But- ter- fly! I'll sing you a song if you show me how to fly!

Bye, Bye, But- ter- fly! I'll see you in the sky!

2. Sometimes your friends must go,
Even though they love you so.
Just want to let you know
I'll see you by and by.

(repeat first verse)

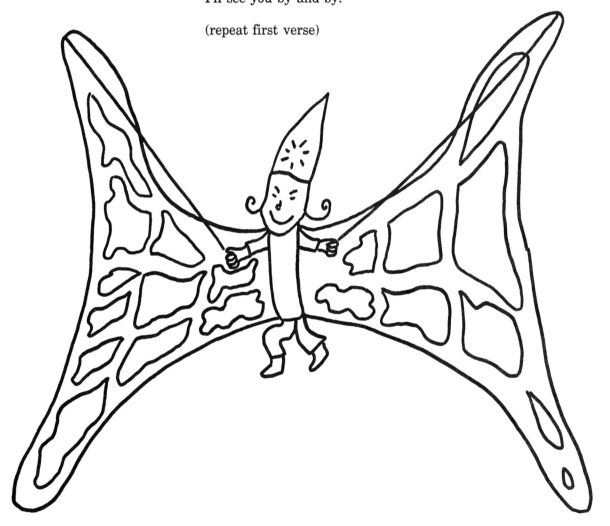

165

Title: **The City Squirrel**

Skills: responds to puppetry; shows curiosity
enjoys singing; moves dramatically
describes personal experiences

Development:

Materials:

A. Awakening . . .

Make a "City Squirrel" handpuppet (see Appendix, pg. 239). Give each child a peanut to feed to the puppet (have the puppet take each nut in its mouth and then place it in a basket, "saving up for winter").

Encourage the children to ask the puppet questions about where it lives, its favorite things to do, the dangers it faces, etc. Respond by having the puppet whisper its answers to you and then relaying them to the children.

puppet pattern
lunch bag
markers
scissors
glue
peanuts
basket

B. Celebrating . . .

Invite the children to learn to sing the song. First, ask them to repeat the line . . .

"You gotta watch out for the hot dog cart!"

. . . whenever it comes around in the song. Gradually, help them to learn the rest of the words through repeated singing.

For variation, encourage the children to move like nervous city squirrels to the music.

C. Embracing . . .

Share the peanuts (see "Awakening") for a "Squirrel Snack." Give each child (ages three and up) a certain number of peanuts and ask them to count them with you. Assist those children who need help breaking the shells open.

Ask the children to relate experiences they have had with the following:

watching/feeding squirrels

visiting a city

playing in a park

peanuts

words and music:
Bob Messano

The City Squirrel

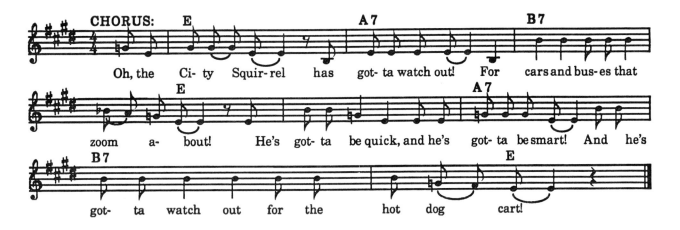

CHORUS: E   A7   B7

Oh, the Ci- ty Squir-rel has got- ta watch out! For cars and bus-es that

E   A7

zoom a- bout! He's got- ta be quick, and he's got- ta be smart! And he's

B7   E

got- ta watch out for the hot dog cart!

2. There's motorcycles, taxis, trucks and trains,
A big bulldozer and a noisy crane!
There's people on the sidewalks and bicycles, too . . .
The City Squirrel wished he was a kangaroo!

(CHORUS)

3. Now, the park is quiet on a Saturday,
'Til the little children come to play!
And old Mrs. Jones, who brings him seeds . . .
'Cause a little bit a'love is all that he needs!

(CHORUS)

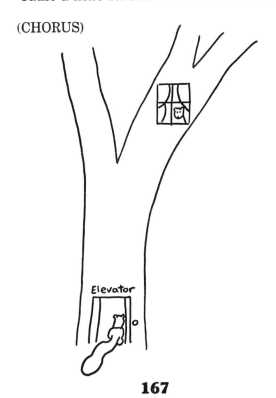

Elevator

Title: **Come In**

Skills: responds to riddles
plays a dramatic role
participates in a celebration

Development: | **Materials:**

A. Awakening . . .

Ask the following riddle:

words to riddle

> *It's a time of stirring spoons,*
> *Going ting-ting against the pots,*
> *A time of sizzle sounds,*
> *As things start getting hot,*
> *A time of scrumptious smells,*
> *That make our tummies tingle,*
> *A time for washing hands,*
> *And helping set the table!*

> *What time is it?* (suppertime/mealtime)

B. Celebrating . . .

Invite the children to play a dramatic musical game, as follows: none
Ask some of the children to pretend to be guests who are coming to a dinner party. Suggest that they go outside the classroom with another teacher until the other children, the hosts, invite them in by singing.
Encourage the hosts to welcome their guests with song and make-believe food, Trade places and repeat.

C. Embracing . . .

Let the children be the hosts of a "Family Pot Luck Dinner" at the   note to parents
school. Send home a note to parents asking them to choose a   copies of song
category of food to bring (see pg. 240).
Arrange for the children to perform the song to welcome their parents to the celebration. Give each parent a copy of the song, suggesting that the children be encouraged to teach it to friends and relatives.

words and music:
Bob Messano

Come In

Come in! Come in! It's ver-y nice to see you! Sit down! Sit down! Sup-per's al-most done!

2. We'll stir it and stir it,
   Put in a little pepper!
   We'll stir it and stir it,
   Supper's almost done!

3. We'll taste and taste it,
   And share it with each other!
   We'll taste it and taste it,
   Supper's almost done!

4. We'll slurp it and slurp it,
   And fill our happy tummies!
   We'll slurp it and slurp it,
   And now our supper's done!

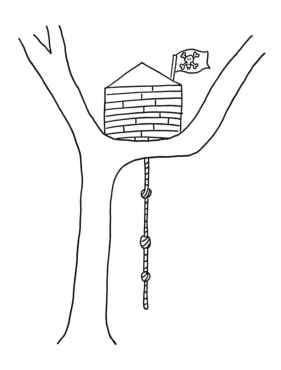

Title: Diggin' in the Mine

Skills: enjoys field strips; responds to riddles
accompanies song with movements; plays imaginatively
uses descriptive language

Development: **Materials:**

A. Awakening . . .

Visit a pet store that sells puppies. Arrange for an employee to   camera
explain the needs of a puppy and name the different breeds. If   film
possible, allow the children to pet them. Take photos of the
children interacting with the animals.
     Ask the following riddle:

> *An old saying says,*
> *I'm man's best friend,*
> *If you throw a stick,*
> *I'll bring it back again!*
>
> *Who am I?* (a puppy/dog)

B. Celebrating . . .

Invite the children to accompany the song by making digging   miner props
motions to the lyrics in the CHORUS.   tape recorder
     Provide the children with a tape of the song plus miner   cassette tape
props, such as the following: hard hats, plastic shovels, flash-
lights, etc. Encourage the children to take turns pretending to be
the miner and the heroic dog in the song.

C. Embracing . . .

Create a bulletin board entitled "We Love Pets!" Ask parents to   photos of pets
lend photos of the children with their pets and include pictures of   markers
the children interacting with pets at the pet store.
     Write down the children's comments about the pets as cap-
tions beneath the photos. Read them back to them on request.

(bluegrass)

words and music:
Bob Messano

Diggin' in the Mine

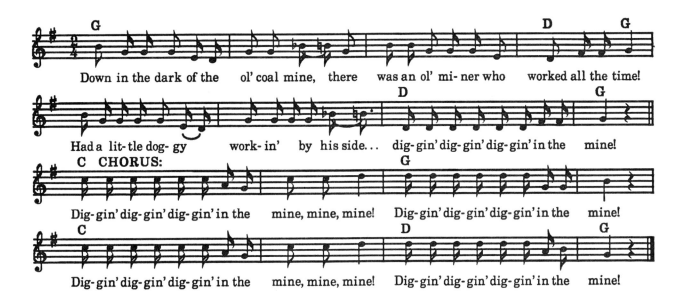

Down in the dark of the ol' coal mine, there was an ol' mi-ner who worked all the time!

Had a lit-tle dog-gy work-in' by his side... dig-gin' dig-gin' dig-gin' in the mine!

CHORUS:

Dig-gin' dig-gin' dig-gin' in the mine, mine, mine! Dig-gin' dig-gin' dig-gin' in the mine!

Dig-gin' dig-gin' dig-gin' in the mine, mine, mine! Dig-gin' dig-gin' dig-gin' in the mine!

2. The roof come down with a tumblin' sound,
A terrible cave-in underground!
But the poor ol' miner and the little hound . . .
Were diggin' diggin' diggin' in the mine!

(CHORUS)

3. They were trapped in the mine far below,
The miner couldn't breathe no more!
But the little doggy followed her nose . . .
Diggin' diggin' diggin' in the mine!

(CHORUS)

4. She dug a tunnel, she dug a hole,
She worked just like a little mole!
Saved the miner and his coal . . .
Diggin' diggin' diggin' in the mine!

(CHORUS)

Title: He Sowed Seed

Skills: listens with interest
sings with spirit; plays tamborine
participates in a celebration

Development: **Materials:**

A. Awakening . . .

Introduce the song with the following story: words to story

Once there was a man named Martin Luther King. He told the people of America about a wonderful dream. In the dream, he saw children from all over the world playing together on a mountain. There was a tall, beautiful tree on the mountain. It was called the Tree of Love!

Martin Luther King took the seeds from that tree and sowed them for you and me . . .

B. Celebrating . . .

Invite the children to sing the song in a lively manner, like an   seed packets
old-time gospel song. Teach them to give the response: *"He sowed a seed!"* throughout the song. Gradually, help them learn the rest of the words through repeated singing.

For variation, provide seed packets which the children can shake in time to the music. These homemade instruments tie in nicely with the song lyrics!

C. Embracing . . .

Have a Martin Luther King celebration! Provide a variety of   multi-cultural
activities that children can choose from, in several learning ar-   materials
eas. For example:

Art: Make a giant rainbow collage on which the children can stick cutout faces of people from around the world.

Language Arts: Ask parents to loan dolls from various cultures. Create an exhibit for the children to experience and discuss.

Science: Plant flower seeds to make the world brighter!

(gospel)

words and music:
Bob Messano

He Sowed a Seed

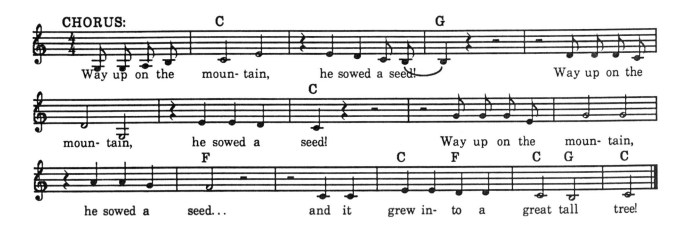

CHORUS:

Way up on the moun- tain, he sowed a seed! Way up on the moun- tain, he sowed a seed! Way up on the moun- tain, he sowed a seed... and it grew in- to a great tall tree!

1. It's the "Tree of Love," he sowed a seed!
It's the "Tree of Love," he sowed a seed!
It's the "Tree of Love," he sowed a seed . . .
And he said there's a place for me!

(CHORUS)

2. It's the "Tree of Peace," he sowed a seed!
It's the "Tree of Peace," he sowed a seed!
It's the "Tree of Peace," he sowed a seed . . .
And he said there's a place for me!

(CHORUS)

3. It's the "Tree of Hope," he sowed a seed!
It's the "Tree of Hope," he sowed a seed!
It's the "Tree of Hope," he sowed a seed . . .
And he said there's a place for me!

(CHORUS)

173

Title: **If I Were an Apple . . .**

Skills: enjoys field trips
dances to music; plays cooperatively
animates a work of edible art

Development: **Materials:**

A. Awakening . . .

Visit the produce section of the supermarket, a neighborhood   apples
fruit stand, or an orchard. Let the children pick apples to bring   basket/bowl
back to the classroom. Teach the children the names of the various varieties (Rome, Mac Intosh, Granny Smith, Delicious, etc.).
Ask the children to help wash and dry the apples. Place
them in a basket or bowl for later use (see "Embracing").

B. Celebrating . . .

Invite the children to play a cooperative game, as follows: pendant pattern
Make necklaces with red, green and yellow apple-pendants   scissors
(see pg. 241). Let the children choose a necklace and ask them to   hole puncher
wear it as they dance to the music.   yarn
Encourage the children to form "apple trees" by inviting
other children to hold hands and dance with them.

C. Embracing . . .

Let the children create some lively "Apple People!" Give each   apples
child an apple and a plastic spoon. Provide bowls of peanut butter   spoons
and bowls of cereal for the children to share. Encourage them to   bowls
spread some peanut butter on their apple and apply cereal to   peanut butter
create eyes, nose, mouth, ears, etc.   cereal
Help the children to recognize the unique aspects of their
creations. Encourage them to eat their edible art.

words and music:
Bob Messano

If I Were an Apple . . .

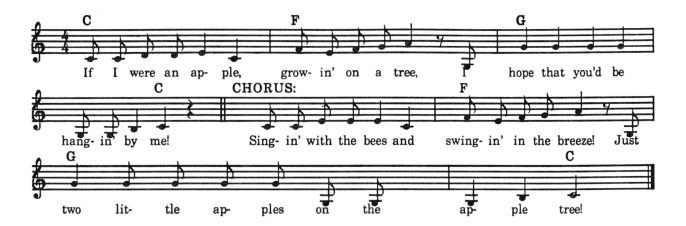

2. If I were yellow and you were green . . .
   It wouldn't really matter to me!

   (CHORUS)

3. Catchin' all the raindrops, dryin' in the sun . . .
   Watchin' all the birdies, havin' lots of fun!

   (CHORUS)

4. We'll turn red when the leaves turn brown . . .
   The wind is blowin', so don't fall down!

   (CHORUS)

   (repeat first verse and CHORUS)

Title: I Like You Very Much

Skills: responds to poetry

sings softly; touches others in a friendly manner

shares music with parents

Development:

Materials:

A. Awakening . . .

Share the following poem:

words to poem
paper
marker

> *I like you . . .*
> *When you smile from ear to ear!*
> *I like you . . .*
> *Whenever you appear!*
> *From up in a tree, or around the block,*
> *Waving from a window, or jumping off a rock!*
> *I like you, it's true,*
> *And I hope you like me, too!*

Invite the children to help you add to the poem by telling what they like to do with friends. Write down their ideas!

B. Celebrating . . .

Invite the children to whisper the song to someone who is sitting near to them. Praise them for touching each other in a gentle, friendly manner.

Adapt the song for various situations by creating new verses. For example, after someone has given you something:

> *I thank you very much!*
> *I thank you very much!*
> *I like to whisper in your ear . . .*
> *I thank you very much!*

C. Embracing . . .

Send home a Music-Gram with the words to the song and some ideas about using gentle music to evoke gentleness in children (see pg. vi).

Music-Gram

Ask parents for feedback about the newsletter and the ways that they share special times with their children. Make them aware of caring, gentle actions that their child has performed at school.

words and music:
Bob Messano

I Like You Very Much

I like you ver- y much! I · like you ver- y much! I like to whis- per

in your ear... I like you ve- ry much!

2. I want to be your friend!
   I want to be your friend!
   I like to whisper in your ear . . .
   I want to be your friend!

3. I want to play with you!
   I want to play with you!
   I like to whisper in your ear . . .
   I want to play with you!

(repeat first verse)

Title: I'm Jumpin'

Skills: listens with interest

demonstrates large-muscle coordination; plays cooperatively

re-creates games; adapts song lyrics

Development: **Materials:**

A. Awakening . . .

Introduce the song with the following story: words to story

Once there was a boy named Jumping Jack. He jumped from morning until night, and he even jumped on the bed. His parents were worried about him, so they took him to the doctor.

The doctor took the boy in the office to look him over. Ten minutes later the door opened. Out came Jumping Jack, and he was jumping higher than ever. Out came the doctor, and he was jumping, too!

"Well, doctor," asked Jack's parents, "why does he jump so much?" The doctor laughed and said, "Because it's fun!"

B. Celebrating . . .

Play a cooperative game as follows: none

Choose one child to start the game. Ask the child to listen for the word *"Stop!"* in the song, and to find a friend to jump with when they hear it. Sing the song while the first child jumps up and down, stops, and chooses a friend. Continue, letting each new child choose a friend, and so on . . .

When about half of the children have been picked, ask everyone to go find a friend and for anyone who wants to jump to do so.

C. Embracing . . .

Make a tape of the song available for the children to originate   tape recorder
their own games. Provide guidance to help children feel included   cassette tape
in the games.

Praise the children for playing cooperatively. Encourage them to adapt the song. For example:

I'm skippin'! I'm skippin'!
I'm skippin' all around!
I'm skippin'! I'm skippin'!
I'm skippin' into town!

words and music:
Bob Messano

I'm Jumpin'

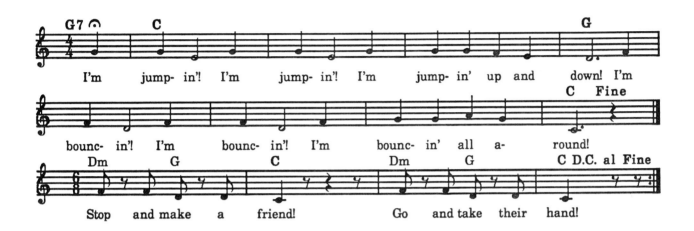

I'm jump-in'! I'm jump-in'! I'm jump-in' up and down! I'm

bounc-in'! I'm bounc-in'! I'm bounc-in' all a-round!

Stop and make a friend! Go and take their hand!

179

Title: **Johnny Appleseed**

Skills: dramatizes poetry
enjoys singing; enjoys dress-up play
participates in a celebration

Development: **Materials:**

A. Awakening . . .

Invite the children to act out the following dramatic-poem: words to poem

> *Old creaking apple tree,*
> *Why are you so blue?*
> *Remember all the children*
> *Who used to play with you . . .*
>
> *Stretch out your branches, now,*
> *And shiver in the sky,*
> *The apple pickers are comin',*
> *To fill their baskets high!*

B. Celebrating . . .

Read the words of the song to the children. Ask them to fill in the   straw hats
words, "Johnny Appleseed," as you sing the song. Help them to   sacks
gradually learn the rest of the words through repeated singing.   fake beard
    For variation, let the children take turns dressing up as   pattern
Johnny Appleseed. Provide straw hats and fake beards for them   hole puncher
to wear (see Appendix pg. 242). Suggest that the children who are   yarn
playing Johnny Appleseed mimic sowing seeds as they stroll to
the music.

C. Embracing . . .

Have a Johnny Appleseed celebration! Let the children partici-   apples and
pate in a variety of cooking projects involving apples. For exam-   other
ple, make: applesauce, baked apples, apple pie, etc.   ingredients
    Invite parents to enjoy the foods the children have created.   cookbook/recipe
    Arrange for the children to perform the song for their par-   charts
ents, complete with costumes.   cooking utensils
                                                                       straw hats
                                                                       sacks
                                                                       fake beards

words and music:
Bob Messano

(narratively)

Johnny Appleseed

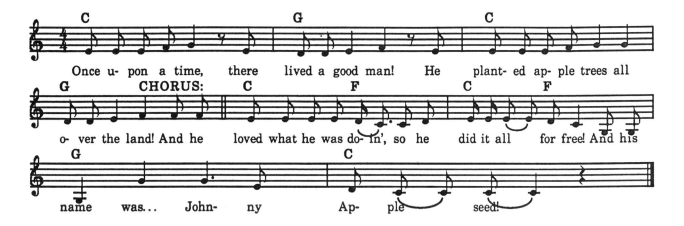

Once u- pon a time, there lived a good man! He plant- ed ap- ple trees all o- ver the land! And he (CHORUS:) loved what he was do- in', so he did it all for free! And his name was... John- ny Ap- ple seed!

2. He walked down the road, makin' things grow,
   All around the valley of the Ohio!

   (CHORUS)

3. They grew so fast, and they grew so tall,
   Turnin' green in the summer, and red in the fall!

   (CHORUS)

4. He planted 'em in the east, he planted 'em in the west,
   And all of the farmers said they were the best!

   (CHORUS)

5. So when you pick an apple, think of what he's done,
   Sharin' such a lovely fruit with everyone!

   (CHORUS)

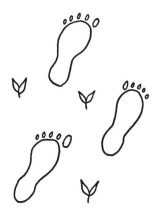

181

Title: **Let's Make a Pancake**

Skills: listens with interest; expresses "likes"
performs a sequence of interpretive body-movements
enjoys field trips

Development: **Materials:**

A. Awakening . . .

Introduce the song with the following story: words to story

*Once there was a place called Pancake Town. Of course, the only
thing to eat in Pancake Town was pancakes! You could spend a
whole week there and never eat the same kind twice. On Monday
there were banana pancakes, on Tuesday there were blueberry
pancakes, on Wednesday there were apple pancakes, on Thursday
there were potato pancakes, on Friday there were whole wheat
pancakes, on Saturday there were silver-dollar pancakes, and on
Sunday there were strawberry pancakes.*
Which kind would you choose?

B. Celebrating . . .

Invite the children to act out the following sequence of actions to   none
accompany the song lyrics:

Verse 1: clap hands; pretend to cook pancakes
Verse 2: make a stirring motion with index finger; say "OUCH!"
Verse 3: pretend to flip pancakes; point to ceiling
Verse 4: pretend to climb ladder; fall down
Verse 5: clap hands; pretend to give pancakes to someone

C. Embracing . . .

Adapt the song for a visit to a pizza parlor, as follows: none

Let's make a pizza, slap it around in our hands!
Let's make a pizza, slap it around in our hands!
Let's make a pizza, just like the pizza-man!

Arrange for the pizza-maker to demonstrate his/her art to the
children. Let the children enjoy a pizza lunch afterwards!

182

(rockin' blues)

words and music:
Bob Messano

Let's Make a Pancake

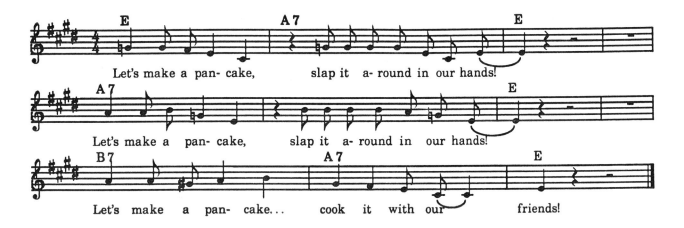

Let's make a pan- cake, slap it a- round in our hands!

Let's make a pan- cake, slap it a- round in our hands!

Let's make a pan- cake... cook it with our friends!

2. Let's put in the butter, the pan is sizzlin' hot! OUCH!
   Let's put in the butter, the pan is sizzlin' hot! OUCH!
   Let's put in the butter, the pan is sizzlin' hot! OUCH!

3. Let's flip our pancakes, flip 'em up in the air!
   Let's flip our pancakes, flip 'em up in the air!
   Let's flip our pancakes, uh-oh, they're stuck up there!

4. Let's climb up the ladder and get those pancakes down!
   Let's climb up the ladder and get those pancakes down!
   Let's climb up the ladder, then we all fall down!

5. Let's make a pancake, slap it around in our hands!
   Let's make a pancake, slap it around in our hands!
   Let's make a pancake, share it with our friends!

183

Title: **Let's Play Our Guitars**

Skills: enjoys field trips
performs a sequence of body movements using props
communicates with a classroom guest

Development: **Materials:**

A. Awakening . . .

Visit a music store which carries a variety of guitars. Arrange for   none
an employee to demonstrate the different qualities of sounds
produced by the following types: steel-string acoustic/folk guitar,
nylon-string classical guitar, electric guitar, etc. Encourage the
children to make comments and ask questions.
   Back in the classroom, ask the children which kind of guitar
they liked the best and why.

B. Celebrating . . .

Invite the children to pantomime the actions of a guitar player   cardboard
and to use their bodies to express the series of sounds in the song.   guitar
   For variation, let the children play cardboard representa-   hole puncher
tions of guitars to accompany the song. Place these guitars in the
"Music-Making Area" of the classroom for the children's sponta-   nylon cord
neous use.

C. Embracing . . .

Invite a parent, friend, music student, professional, etc., to visit   camera
the classroom and share some guitar-playing. Prepare the chil-   film
dren for the visitor, explaining that the visitor has a special
talent to share. Ask them if they know any musically talented
people at home.
   Take photos of the children's interaction with the visitor
and place on a bulletin board for parents.

184

words and music:
Bob Messano

Let's Play Our Guitars

Let's play our gui-tars! Let's play our gui-tars!

Variations:

Boing-Boing-Boing-Boing-Boing! (4x)

Zing-Zing-Zing-Zing-Zing! (4x)

Let's all play 'em fast! (4x)

Shooby-dooby-dooby-doo! (4x)

(etc.)

Title: **Native American Song**

Skills: responds to poetry

enjoys dancing and playing rhythm instruments

explores Native America lifestyles through dolls

Development:

Materials:

A. Awakening . . .

Share the following poem:

words to poem

The earth is like a grandmother . . .
When we are hungry she gives us food,
If we are cold she gives us wood for our fires,
When we are thirsty she gives us clear springs.
The sky is like a loving grandfather . . .
Sending down precious sunlight, rain, and snow,
Holding stars and clouds and birds in his great arms,
Giving us air to breathe every second of every day.
Let us be thankful for the earth and sky,
And listen to them carefully,
Like we do to our own grandparents!

Ask the children what they would say to the earth and sky if they could talk with them.

B. Celebrating . . .

Invite the children to learn the words of the chant. When they are familiar with the words, encourage them to take turns dancing and playing instruments representative of traditional Native American instruments, including: rasps, drums, rattles, etc.

Let the children design their own Native American costumes and perform the song for other children in the school (see pg. 243).

rhythm instruments

paper grocery bags

scissors

assorted art materials

glue

C. Embracing . . .

Make a set of clothespin dolls representing Native American people (see pg. 243). Encourage the children to play with the dolls and to create imaginative stories about the people.

Suggest that the children use blocks or other available materials to represent the people's homes, villages, canoes, etc.

Provide clothespins and art materials for the children to make their own dolls.

clothespins

assorted art materials

glue

blocks

186

words and music:
Bob Messano

Native American Song

2. One circle, for all our people!
   One circle, for all our friends!
   One circle, for all our people!
   One circle, for all our friends!

   (CHORUS)

3. One forest, for all our people!
   One forest, for all our friends!
   One forest, for all our people!
   One forest, for all our friends!

   (CHORUS)

4. One ocean, for all our people!
   One ocean, for all our friends!
   One ocean, for all our people!
   One ocean, for all our friends!

   (CHORUS)

5. One planet, for all our people!
   One planet, for all our friends!
   One planet, for all our people!
   One planet, for all our friends!

   (CHORUS)

Title: **A New Thanksgiving Song**

Skills: responds to poetry

enjoys singing; dances to music

expresses thanks for food

Development: **Materials:**

A. Awakening . . .

Introduce the song with the following poem: paper
marker

When all of the fruits of the harvest are in . . .
When all the world's people can live as friends . . .
When all the good things are where they belong . . .
It's then we'll be singing . . .
A New Thanksgiving Song!

Ask the children to help make a list of things they are thankful
for. Read it back to them.

B. Celebrating . . .

Invite the children to pretend to be Native American dancers!   paper
Encourage them to decorate paper headbands by taping on feath-   headbands
ers and to wear them as they dance to the music.   feathers
    Suggest that they dance around an imaginary fire, indicated   tape
by a circle of orange traffic cones, a red hula hoop, etc.   traffic cones,
hula hoop

C. Embracing . . .

Teach the children to say a few words of thanks before each meal.   words to grace
For example:

Thanks for our families
Who help us to grow;
Thanks for the love
Of the people we know!

Talk about all the people who have helped bring the food from the
earth to the table, including: farmers, truck drivers, supermarket
workers, family, etc.

words and music:
Bob Messano

A New Thanksgiving Song

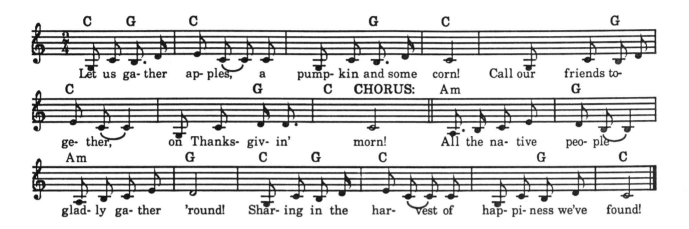

Let us ga- ther ap- ples, a pump- kin and some corn! Call our friends to-ge- ther, on Thanks- giv- in' morn! CHORUS: All the na- tive peo- ple glad- ly ga- ther 'round! Shar- ing in the har- vest of hap- pi- ness we've found!

2. Listen to the fiddle,
   The pretty mandolin!
   See the children dancing . . .
   Let the fun begin!

   (CHORUS)

3. Help to set the table,
   Fill the glasses high!
   Smile at all your neighbors . . .
   As they're passin' by!

   (CHORUS)

4. Squirrels are in the treetops,
   The geese are flyin' home!
   Everyone is singin' . . .
   A New Thanksgiving' Song!

   (CHORUS)

   (repeat first verse and CHORUS)

Title: Panda Played Piano

Skills: listens with interest
plays a dramatic role; using props
makes musical experiments

Development:	**Materials:**

A. Awakening . . .

Introduce the song with the following story:

words to story

Once there was a Musical Zoo and just about every animal there could play an instrument. All except Panda, that is. Her big paws made it very hard for her to play anything. Monkey gave Panda a piano to practice on, but Panda had a hard time with it. One day, a little boy came to Panda's den. He was lost and very sad. Panda felt so sorry for the little boy that she played her brightest, happiest song for him and pretty soon he wasn't so sad anymore. "That sounded like a sunny day!" he said. Panda was thrilled and kept on playing 'til the boy's mother came running up with the zookeeper. And Panda's been playing sunny days and blue skies ever since . . .

B. Celebrating . . .

Invite the children to pantomime the instrument-playing animals in the song.

instruments

For variation, let the children play instruments which correspond to the instruments in the song. For example:

Panda's Piano: xylophone or piano
Hippo's Trumpet: cardboard tube kazoo
Gorilla's Drums: coffee can/oatmeal carton drums
Monkey's Guitar: box-and-rubber-band guitar

C. Embracing . . .

Create a "Music-Making Area" in the classroom where the children can freely explore and experiment with music, including: playing instruments, acting out songs with puppets and props, listening to records and tapes, etc.

musical materials

Place the materials so they are arranged in an attractive, orderly way, and are easily accessible to the children. Give the children the opportunity to use the materials on a daily basis.

words and music:
Bob Messano

Panda Played Piano

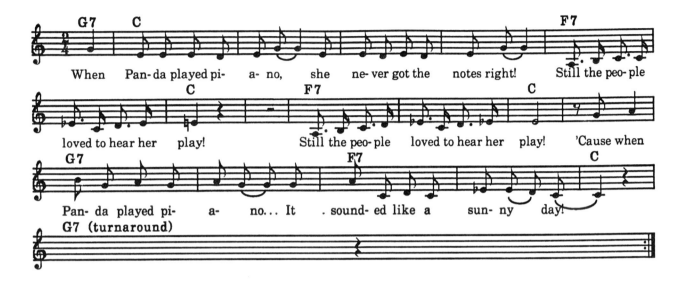

When Pan-da played pi-a-no, she ne-ver got the notes right! Still the peo-ple loved to hear her play! Still the peo-ple loved to hear her play! 'Cause when Pan-da played pi-a-no... It sound-ed like a sun-ny day!

G7 (turnaround)

2. When Hippo played the trumpet . . .

3. When Gorilla played the drums . . .

4. When Monkey played the guitar . . .

Title: **A Quiet Place**

Skills: responds to poetry; relates to a hearing-impaired person
leads others in a game
enjoys quiet activities

Development: **Materials:**

A. Awakening . . .

Share the following poem: words to poem

> *A boy was born who could not hear,*
> *Either the music of the stream,*
> *Or the running of the deer.*
> *But he watched these things,*
> *And as he grew,*
> *He learned the signs,*
> *To tell what he knew.*
> *And if you think about it,*
> *You'll see he was wise,*
> *For there are two ways to listen . . .*
> *With our ears and with our eyes!*

Invite a hearing-impaired person to meet the children and communicate with them through sign language, play, dance, etc.

B. Celebrating . . .

Ask the children to try expressing some of the following concepts using wordless gestures and body movements:
Stop
I'm hurt
Love
Sleep
Scared
Quiet
Encourage them to invent gestures to accompany the song.

C. Embracing . . .

Create a "Quiet Place" in the classroom. Place comfortable cush-   quiet materials
ions, stuffed animals, an inviting rug, puzzles, etc., in this area.
Encourage the children to use soft voices when they are playing
there.
Suggest that children who become disruptive in other classroom areas spend some time in the "Quiet Place" until they feel
ready to cooperate again. Encourage the children to discuss their
feelings about their behavior in this area.

words and music:
Bob Messano

A Quiet Place

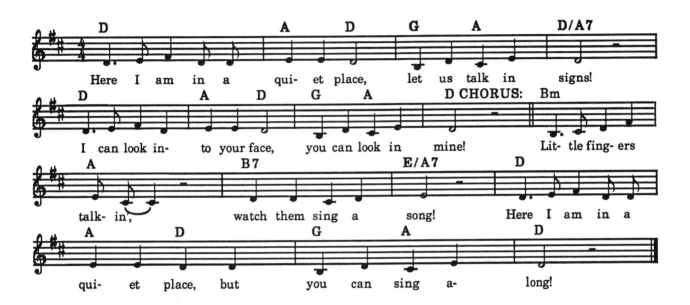

Here I am in a qui- et place, let us talk in signs!
I can look in- to your face, you can look in mine! Lit- tle fing- ers
talk- in', watch them sing a song! Here I am in a
qui- et place, but you can sing a- long!

2. Here I am in a quiet place,
Wondering what to do!
I can see a friendly face,
Someone just like you!

(CHORUS)

3. Here we are in a quiet place,
Talking with our hands!
Everytime that we embrace,
I know that we are friends!

(CHORUS)

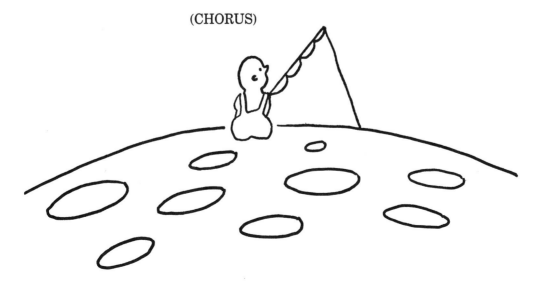

193

Title: **Sam the Clam's Blues**

Skills: responds to puppetry; shows concern for environment
enjoys singing; makes and plays instruments
participates in a celebration

Development:

Materials:

A. Awakening . . .

Make a *Sam the Clam* hand puppet (see Appendix pg. 244). Have the puppet talk to the children about how unhappy he is when people litter and pollute the sea. Show them samples of trash that litter our beaches. For example: a soda can, a candy wrapper, plastic six-pack holders, etc.

   Ask the children what they think people should do with their trash instead of leaving it at the beach.

puppet pattern
lunch bag
scissors
markers
glue
litter samples

B. Celebrating . . .

Invite the children to learn *Sam the Clam's* part in the song (the CHORUS). Help them to gradually learn the rest of the words through repeated singing.

   Let them make homemade instruments from recycled materials to accompany the song. For example, they can: fill plastic shampoo bottles with rice for shakers, decorate oatmeal cartons for drums, etc.

recycled
   materials

C. Embracing . . .

Have a "Clean Earth Concert" where the children play their homemade instruments and sing songs about a beautiful earth (e.g., *"All the Green Things,"* pg. 107). Perform for parents, other classes, or other schools.

   Compliment the children regularly as they clean up the classroom, point out debris in the playground, etc.

homemade
   instruments

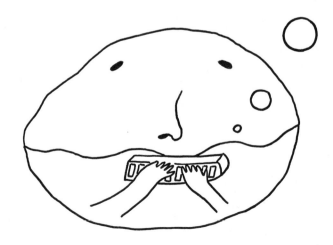

words and music:
Bob Messano

Sam the Clam's Blues

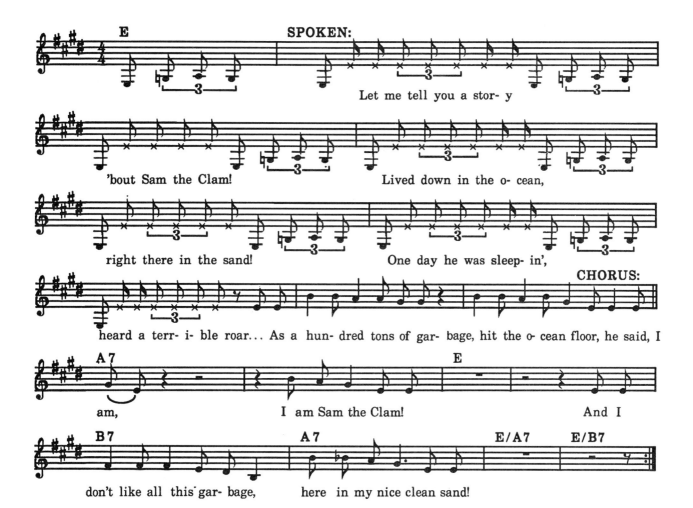

E   SPOKEN:

Let me tell you a stor- y

'bout Sam the Clam!   Lived down in the o- cean,

right there in the sand!   One day he was sleep- in',

CHORUS:

heard a terr- i- ble roar... As a hun- dred tons of gar- bage, hit the o- cean floor, he said, I

A 7   E

am,   I am Sam the Clam!   And I

B 7   A 7   E/A7   E/B7

don't like all this gar- bage,   here in my nice clean sand!

2. There's cans and bottles, there's paper bags,
There's cigarette butts, and oily ol' rags!
It looks unsightly, it smells so bad . . .
I know one little clam, who's gettin' kinda mad!

(CHORUS)

3. So if you go a' walkin', down by the sand,
Please don't litter, use a garbage can!
You'll make somebody happy, everytime you lend a hand . . .
You'll get a personal thank-you, from Sam the Clam!

(CHORUS)

Title: **The Water and the Old Mill Wheel**

Skills: responds to poetry
plays cooperatively; demonstrates large-muscle coordination
uses descriptive language

Development: **Materials:**

A. Awakening . . .

Share the following poem: words to poem

> *There's so many things that a river can do . . .*
> *It can turn a generator and make power for you.*
> *It can feed lots of people with colorful fish,*
> *It'll take you canoeing if that's what you wish.*
> *But the best kind of river just rolls right along . . .*
> *A little bit lazy, and singin' a song!*

Ask the children to describe experiences they have had along
rivers. Whom did they share those experiences with?

B. Celebrating . . .

Make a "river" by placing two sets of traffic cones in concentric   traffic cones
circles (one inside the other). Help the children find partners and   yarn
to hold hands with them. Encourage them to skip along to the
song.

Adapt the song for outdoors by mapping out a "winding
river" with long pieces of yarn laid upon the ground. Challenge
the children to follow the river.

C. Embracing . . .

Make a bulletin board entitled "Doing Things Together." Put up   photos
photographs of the children sharing a variety of cooperative ac-   marker
tivities, such as: setting the snack table, playing ball, pulling
someone in a wagon, etc.

Ask the children to name the people they are sharing/
playing with and to describe what is happening in the pictures.
Write down their words as captions to the photos and read them
back upon request.

words and music:
Bob Messano

The Water and the Old Mill Wheel

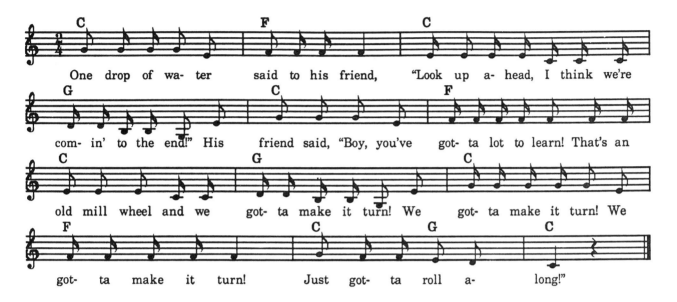

One drop of wa- ter said to his friend, "Look up a- head, I think we're com- in' to the end." His friend said, "Boy, you've got- ta lot to learn! That's an old mill wheel and we got- ta make it turn! We got- ta make it turn! We got- ta make it turn! Just got- ta roll a- long!"

2. They came to the wheel and the wheel was dry,
So they gave a little push and they gave a little try!
The wheel started spinnin' and the water did, too,
And the little drop said, it's easy to do!
It's easy to do, it's easy to do . . .
Just gotta roll along!

3. Now they go together down the river so blue,
The big drop of water and the little one, too!
There ain't a wheel that they can't spin,
If they just stick together like two good friends!
Two good friends, two good friends . . .
Just gotta roll along!

Title: **We Make Music**

Skills: learns and performs sign language sequence
sings and performs signs
teaches a song to others

Development: **Materials:**

A. Awakening . . .

Teach the children the following sequence of sign language signs: none

> We: Point to one shoulder, bring hand across to point to the other shoulder.
>
> Make: Put one fist on top of the other and make a turning motion.
>
> Music: Hold one arm out straight and make a back-and-forth motion with your other hand (like strumming a harp) over it.
>
> Friends: Link pinkies together with yourself or with friends.

B. Celebrating . . .

Invite the children to sing the song, accompanied by the signs   triangles
learned above.
After the children become confident performing the song, add the sound of triangles to their interpretation.
Let them take turns playing the triangles along with the words while others perform the signs.

C. Embracing . . .

Visit another class in the school and let the children teach the   none
song to the children.
Set up a "Song Sharing Time" when different classes can visit one another and teach each other their favorite songs.
Use the song at the closing of each "Song Sharing Time."

words and music:
Bob Messano

We Make Music

We make mu-sic! We make mu-sic! We make mu-sic! We make friends!

Title: **We're Goin' Skatin'**

Skills: names articles of winter dress
performs a sequence of body movements; plays cooperatively
participates in a celebration

Development: **Materials:**

   A. Awakening . . .

       Make a flannelboard ice skater figure with various articles of   flannelboard
       winter dress (see Appendix pg. 245). Let the children take turns   felt pieces
       dressing the skater warmly for a day on the ice. Ask them to
       name each article of clothing they apply.
         Place the figure and the clothes in the "Library/Language
       Area" of the classroom for the children to use independently.
       Encourage them to talk about their own ice skating experiences.

   B. Celebrating . . .

       Invite the children to dress up as ice skaters and act out the   winter clothes
       sequence of body movements in the song. Provide oversized hats,
       scarves, and mittens for a joyous interpretation to ensue.
         Mark off a "skating rink" by making a large circle of colored
       yarn on the floor. Challenge the children to follow one another
       around the inside of the circle or join up with partners as they
       interpret the song.

   C. Embracing . . .

       Have a "Winter Olympics" with various cooperative games and   up to you
       activities. For example, try some of the following:

       Dog Sled Run: Two children pull one child on a sled by
       means of a rope; mark out a racecourse for the children to follow.

       Snow Painting: The children brush colored water on snow
       to create nature pictures.

       Snow Bowl: The children try to knock over plastic milk jugs
       with snowballs.

(boogie woogie)

words and music:
Bob Messano

We're Goin' Skatin'

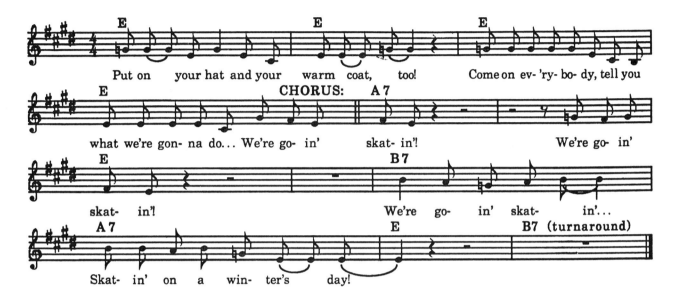

Put on your hat and your warm coat, too! Come on ev-'ry-bo-dy, tell you what we're gon-na do... We're go-in' skat-in'!

CHORUS: A 7

We're go-in' skat-in'!

B 7

We're go-in' skat-in'...

A 7

Skat-in' on a win-ter's day!

E

B7 (turnaround)

2. Skate to the left!
   Skate to the right!
   Slippin' and a'slidin' and we're doin' alright . . .

   (CHORUS)

3. Skate to the front!
   Skate to the back!
   Let's head over to the warm-up shack . . .

   (CHORUS)

   (repeat first verse and CHORUS)

Title: # We Wiggle When We Wash Our Hands

Skills: responds to poetry
does a funny musical walk
takes care of personal hygiene

Development: **Materials:**

A. Awakening . . .

Share the following poem: words to poem

> *Each and every day,*
> *I do my Clean-Up Show.*
> *The shower curtain opens,*
> *And I am set to go . . .*
>
> *I rub my magic soap,*
> *And I wave my magic wand,*
> *Super-Presto-Change-o . . .*
> *And all the dirt is gone!*

Invite the children to join in a "Clean-Up Show" by going to wash
their hands.

B. Celebrating . . .

Sing the song and encourage the children to do a "wiggle walk" on   tape recorder
the way to the "Wash-Up Area."   cassette tape
    Put the song on a tape and play it each day as a transition
time signal (before "Wash-Up Time").
    Adapt the song for other classroom situations. For example:

> *We wiggle when we walk,*
> *And we wiggle when we talk,*
> *And we wiggle when we go outside!*

C. Embracing . . .

Ask the children to help you make a list of things they do at   paper
school *and* at home. For example, the list might include: marker

> *we wash our hands*
>
> *we make friends*
>
> *we get hugs*
>
> *we brush our teeth*
>
> *we take naps*
>
> *we clean up after playing*
>
> *we eat*

Send home periodic newsletters to parents, emphasizing the rela-
tionship between success in school and at home.

words and music:
Bob Messano

We Wiggle When We Wash Our Hands

Oh, we wig- gle when we walk, and we wig- gle when we talk! We wig- gle when we wash our hands!

2. With a little bit of water,
   And a little bit of soap,
   And a little bit of lovin' care!

(repeat first verse)

Title: Who Is Friends with a Cat?

Skills: listens with interest

enjoys singing and dress-up play; treats others kindly

helps create classroom rules

Development: **Materials:**

A. Awakening . . .

Introduce the song with the following story: words to story

*Once there was a most unfriendly cat. Even the dogs were
afraid of her! The mice never came out of their hole when she was
around, and the birds flew to the highest branches of the trees to
stay out of her reach.*

*One day, a little girl came walking down the street where the
cat lived. "Don't go that way!" warned her friends, but she kept on
going anyway. As she walked she sang this song . . .*

B. Celebrating . . .

Invite the children to learn the words to the song. First, ask them   prop pattern
to repeat the phrase, *"Cause you don't get along with anybody!"* at   construction
the end of each verse. Help them to learn the rest of the words   paper
through repeated singing.   scissors
    Let the children make and wear "cat ears" as they move like   stapler
cats to the music (see Appendix pg. 246). Encourage everyone to
give each other a friendly hug at the conclusion of the song!

C. Embracing . . .

Ask the children to help make a list of things they like for people   paper
to do for them, and things they don't like people to do to them.   marker
    From the list, make a set of classroom rules. Create picture
symbols to go along with the words. Reward the class with praise
as they treat each other kindly and help them to modify their
behavior at other times.

(dramatically)

words and music:
Bob Messano

Who Is Friends with a Cat?

Who is friends with a Cat? "Not me!" said the Bird. "Why's that?" said the Cat. " 'Cause you don't get a- long with an- y- bo- dy!

2. Who is friends with a cat?
   "Not me!" said the dog.
   "Why's that?" said the cat.
   "Cause you don't get along with anybody!"

3. Who is friends with a cat?
   "Not me!" said the mouse.
   "Why's that?" said the cat.
   "Cause you don't get along with anybody!"

4. Who is friends with a cat?
   "Not me!" said the bug.
   "Why's that?" said the cat.
   "Cause you don't get along with anybody!"

5. Who is friends with a cat?
   "I am!" said the girl.
   "Why's that?" said the cat.
   "Cause I get along with everybody!"

Title: Will You Be My Cuddly Panda Bear?

Skills: shows imaginative thinking
enjoys dancing
shares music with parents

Development: **Materials:**

A. Awakening . . .

Show the children a picture of a panda bear. Ask them questions,   picture of panda
such as the following: bear

Would you like to hug this animal? Why or why not?

What would you do if you found it in your bathtub?

*What would your parents say if you brought this animal
home from the zoo?*

B. Celebrating . . .

Help the children to find partners and invite them to dance to the   teddy bears
music.

For variation, invite the children to bring in teddy bears
from home. Adapt the song lyrics for the children to dance with
their bears, as follows:

Will you be my cuddly teddy bear?
Will you be my cuddly teddy bear?
If you'll be my teddy bear,
I will take you to the fair!
Will you be my cuddly teddy bear?

C. Embracing . . .

Send home a newsletter to the parents featuring the words to the   Music-Gram
song and suggestions for creating music with children (see pg.
vii).

Ask for feedback from the parents and children about sharing the song at home. For example:

How does it feel to be cuddled?

206

words and music:
Bob Messano

Will You Be My Cuddly Panda Bear?

Will you be my cud-dly pan-da bear? Will you be my cud-dly pan-da bear? If you'll be my pan-da bear... I will be your po-lar bear! Will you be my cud-dly pan-da bear?

2. Will you be my fuzzy caterpillar?
Will you be my fuzzy caterpillar?
If you'll be my caterpillar,
I will be your big goriller . . .
Will you be my fuzzy caterpillar?

3. Will you be my lovely little mouse?
Will you be my lovely little mouse?
If you'll be my little mouse,
I will be your speckled grouse . . .
Will you be my lovely little mouse?

4. Will you be my sweet and shaggy moose?
Will you be my sweet and shaggy moose?
If you'll be my shaggy moose,
I will be your silly goose . . .
Will you be my sweet and shaggy moose?

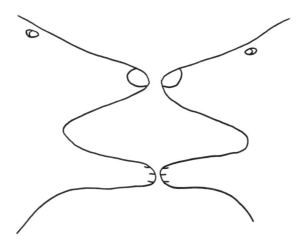

Appendix

Reproducible Patterns and Charts for the Music Activities

Camp Sleepy rebus chart
Giant Steps footprints
In My Home finger puppets
A Little Birdy Told Me stick puppets
The Baseball Boogie pennant
Bees Buzz rebus chart
Happy Blueberry recipe chart
Mr. and Mrs. Mouse party announcement
Octopus, Octopus seascape creatures
Pass Around the Peppermint stick puppets
Put Your PJ's On flannelboard pieces
Rockin' in the Rabbit Hole props
Scrambled Eggs picture-card sequence
So Many Bones hobby-horse head
Suzy Turkey turkey track and stick puppets
Tiger at the Movies silhouette stick puppets
All the Green Things necklace pendants
Betsy Bear bulletin board
Cuckoo Clock time-line of activities

Helicopter flannelboard pieces
The Mud Song hand puppet
The Snow rebus chart
The Snow hand puppets
The Tree's Song music tree
We're in a Spaceship! prop
Bald Eagle hand puppet
Broken Bears props
Bye, Bye, Butterfly stick puppet
The City Squirrel hand puppet
Come In! sample note to parents
If I Were an Apple prop
Johnny Appleseed dress-up prop
Native American Song dress-up prop and
   clothespin tribe
Sam-the-Clam's Blues hand puppet
We're Goin' Skatin' dress-up figure
Who Is Friends with a Cat? dress-up prop

Camp Sleepy
rebus chart

Come into Camp Sleepy
Crawl into my ⛺
Who is up to bring the 🪵
To start the morning 🔥

It's clink-a-clink as mama gets the 🍳
To put the cornmeal in
But I'm way down in my sleepin' sack
Back in ol' Dreamland

Great 🐻 walks in the nighttime
Drums on a hollow 🌳
But I'll be safe
Inside my sack
If he comes lookin' for me

Giant Steps
footprints

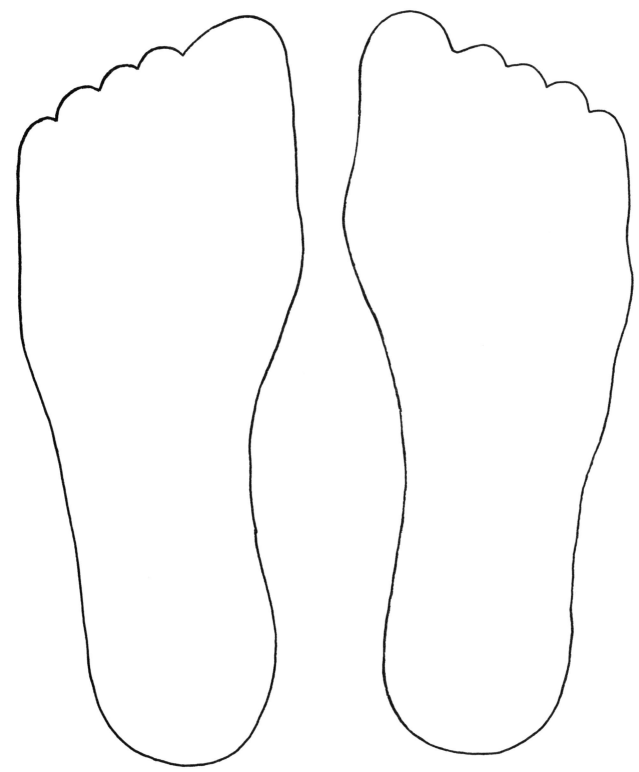

In My Home
finger puppets

mother

father

sister

brother

A Little Birdy Told Me!
stick puppets

The Baseball Boogie
pennant

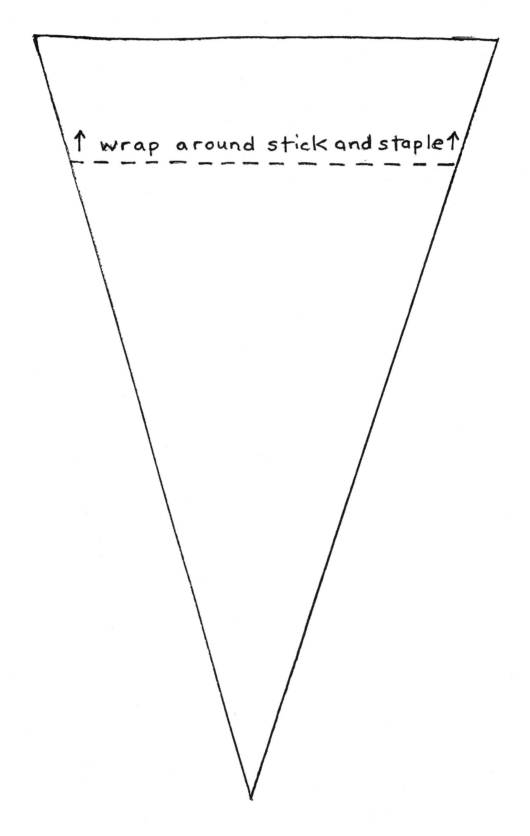

↑ wrap around stick and staple↑

Bees Buzz
rebus chart

buzz in the

buzz on the

buzz in the

buzz on your

215

Happy Blueberry
recipe chart

Blueberries + Milk

1. Put ½ cup of blueberries in a bowl.

2. Add 1 cup of milk.

3. Eat with a spoon.

Mr, + Mrs. Mouse
party announcement

Mouse Party
Today!
No Cats Allowed!
(please wear tails)

attach piece
of yarn for
tail

Octopus, Octopus
seascape creatures

hang by thread here

Pass Around the Peppermint
stick puppets

frog

snake

snail

slug

Put Your PJ's On !
flannelboard pieces

Rockin' in the Rabbit Hole
props

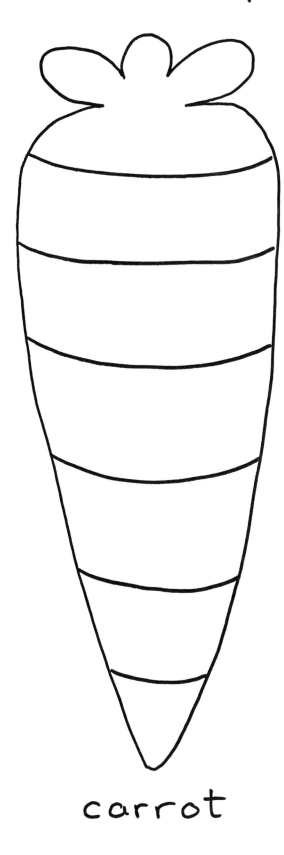

carrot

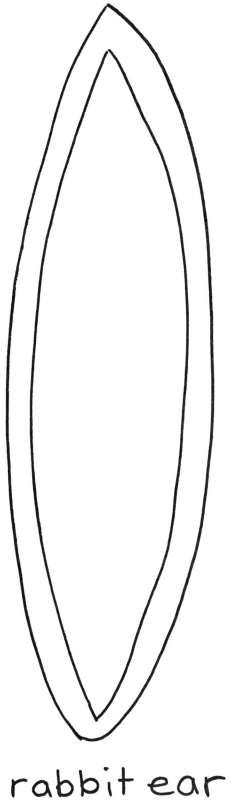

rabbit ear

Scrambled Eggs
picture-card sequence

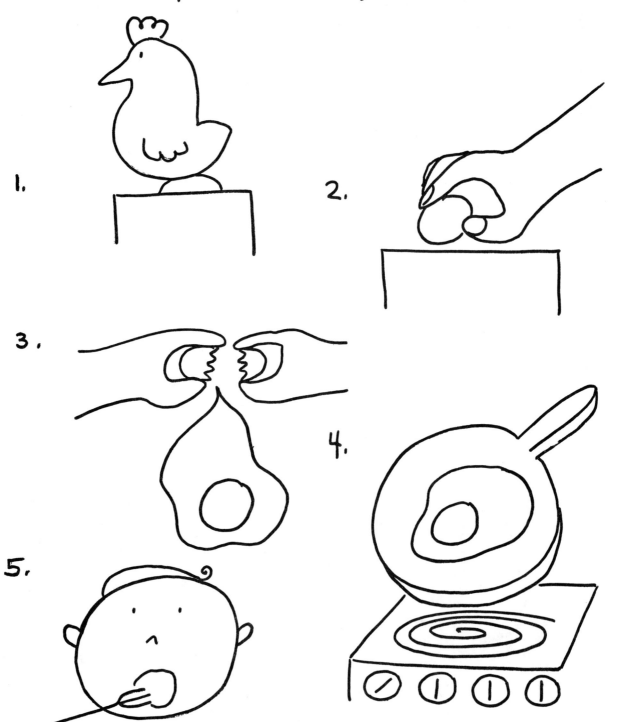

1.

2.

3.

4.

5.

So Many Bones!
hobby-horse head

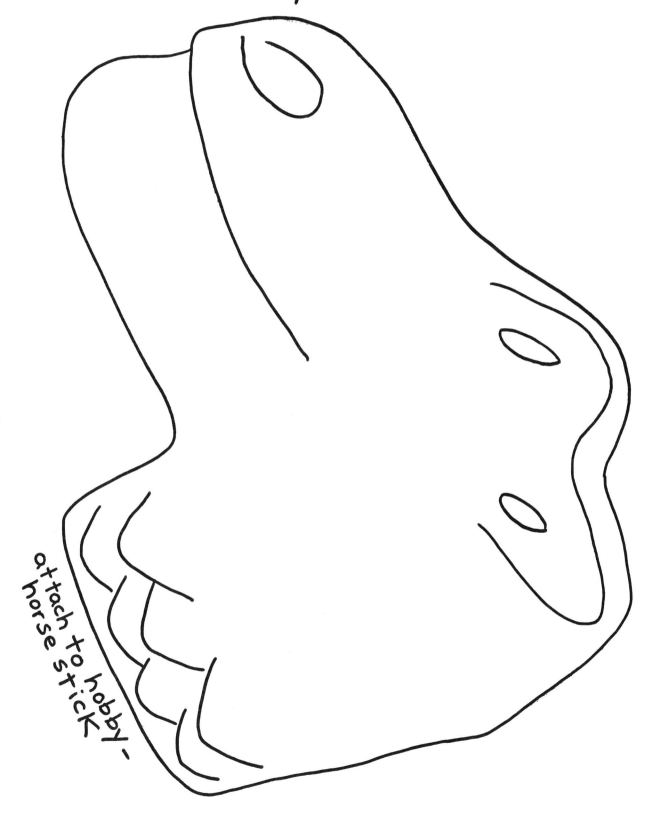

attach to hobby-horse stick

223

Suzy Turkey
turkey track

stick
puppets

Tiger at the Movies
silhouette stick puppets

All the Green Things
necklace pendants

Betsy Bear
bulletin board

The Animals Go to Sleep

Cuckoo Clock
time - line of activities

Helicopter
flannel-board pieces

The Mud Song
hand puppet

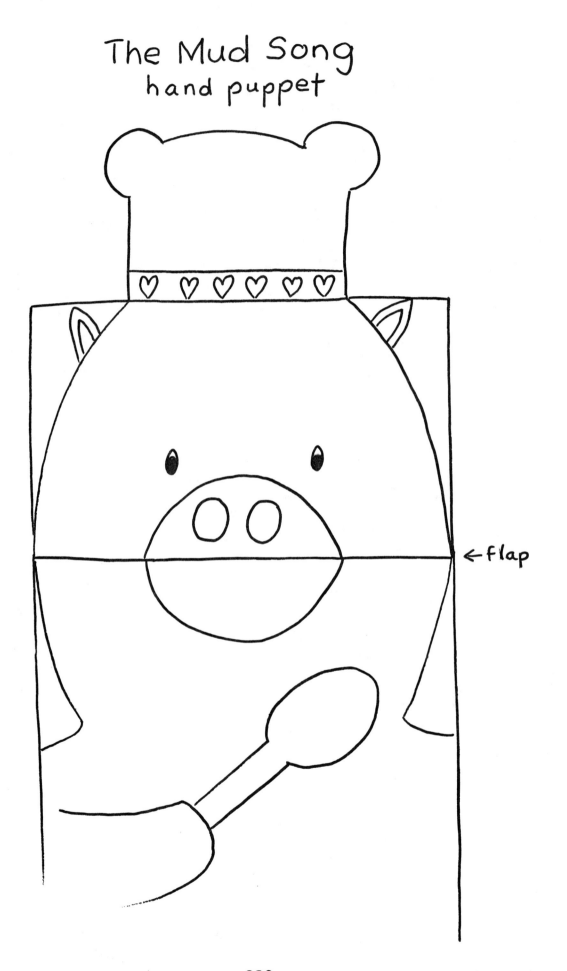

←flap

The Snow
rebus chart

The ❄ is falling on the ⛰

The  ❄ is falling on the 🌳

The  ❄ is falling on the 〰

The  ❄ is falling on 🧑

231

The Snow
hand puppets

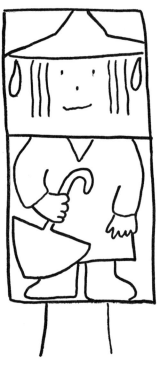

Rainey Janey

Snowy Sam

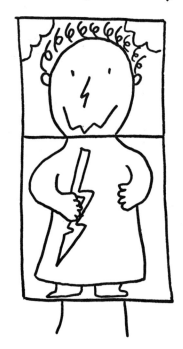

Lightning Lynn

Sunny Sid

232

The Tree's Song
music tree

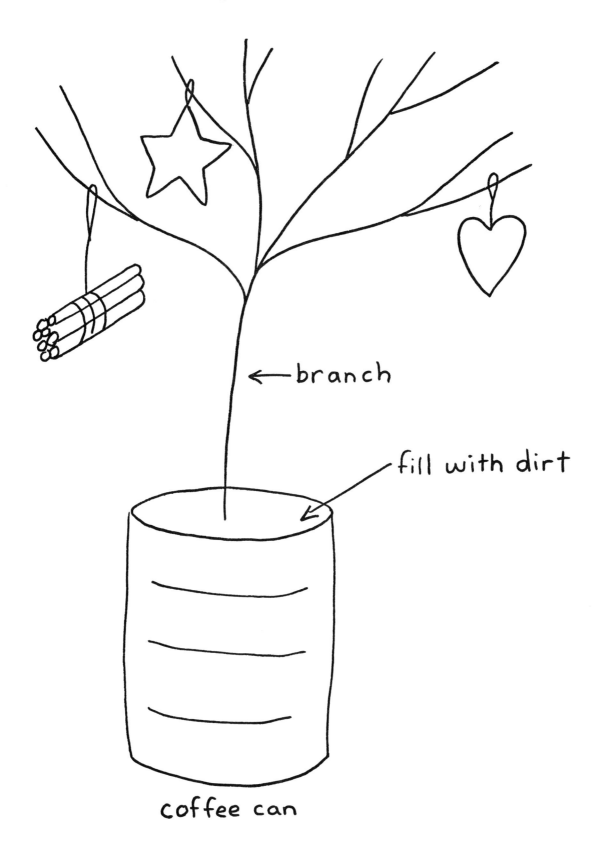

← branch

fill with dirt

coffee can

We're in a Spaceship!

prop

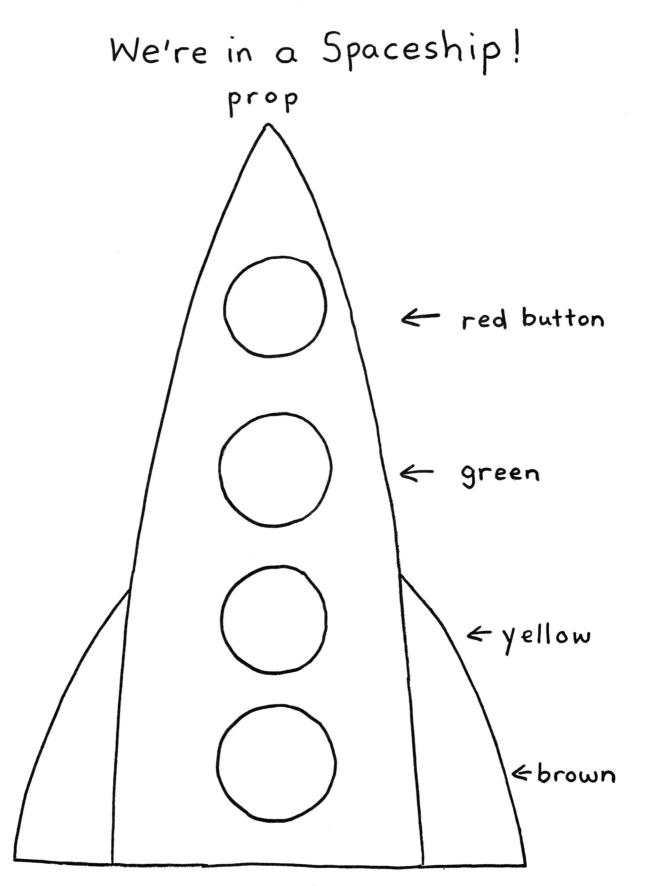

← red button

← green

← yellow

←brown

Bald Eagle
hand puppet

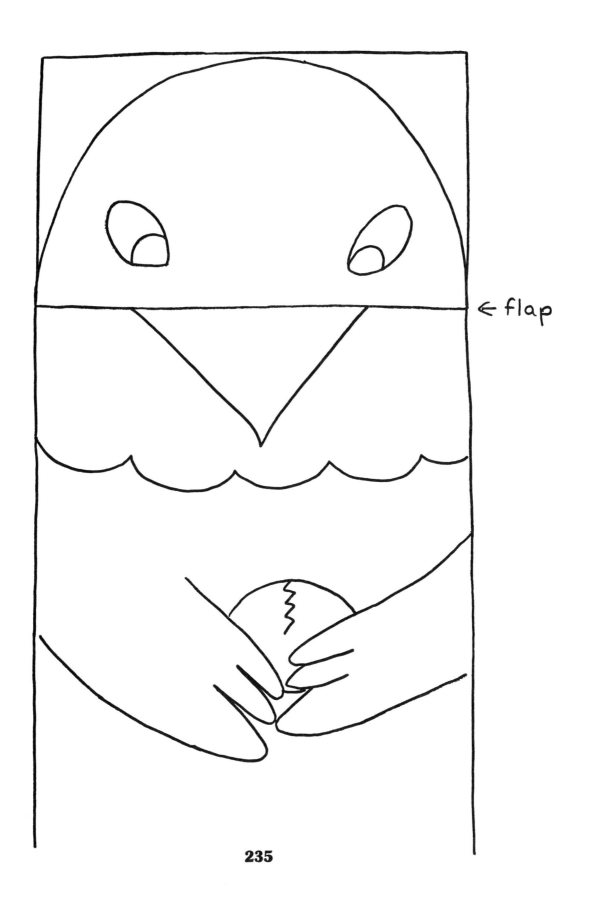

← flap

Broken Bears
prop

Broken Bears
prop

Hospital

Bye, Bye, Butterfly!
stick puppet

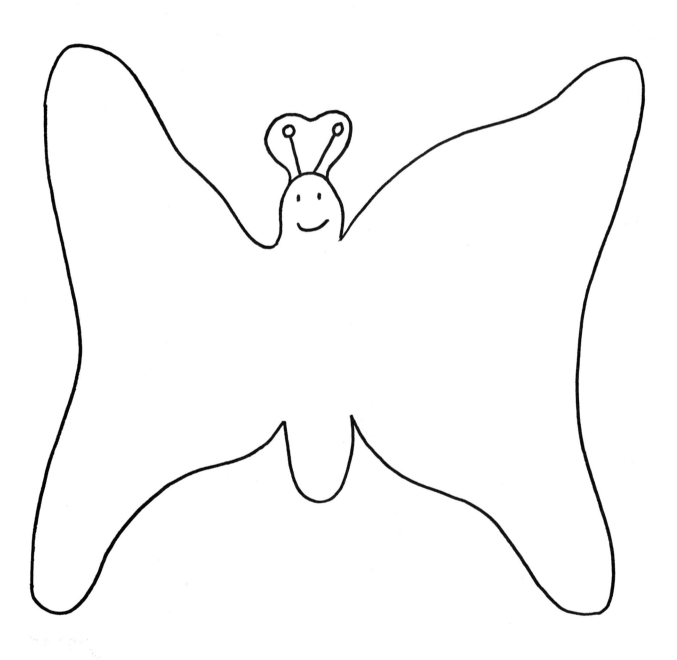

The City Squirrel
hand puppet

Come In !

sample note to parents

You're
invited
to our

Pot
Luck

Dinner !

Our class will be hosting a Pot Luck Dinner on

_____

at _____ .

Please check off one category of food that you will be able to provide Thanks and see you there !

Name: _____

☐ Main Course

☐ Side Dish

☐ Appetizer

☐ Salad

☐ Dessert

☐ Other, please describe
_____

Return this form as soon as possible!

If I Were An Apple
prop

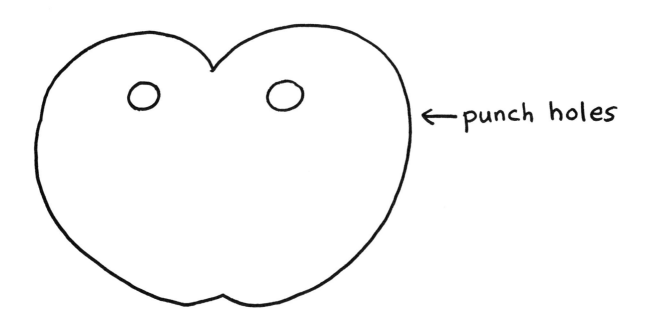

← punch holes

Johnny Appleseed
dress-up prop

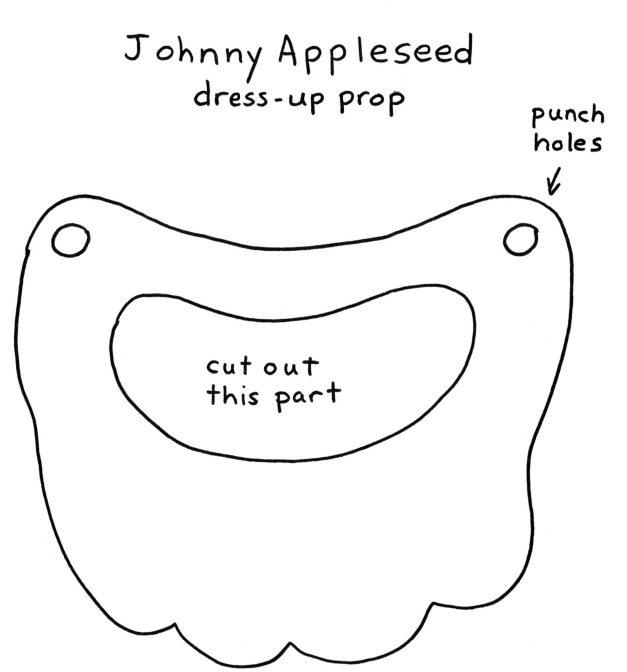

punch
holes

cut out
this part

Native American Song
dress-up prop

paper grocery
bag

Native American Song
clothespin tribe

Sam-the-Clam's Blues
hand puppet

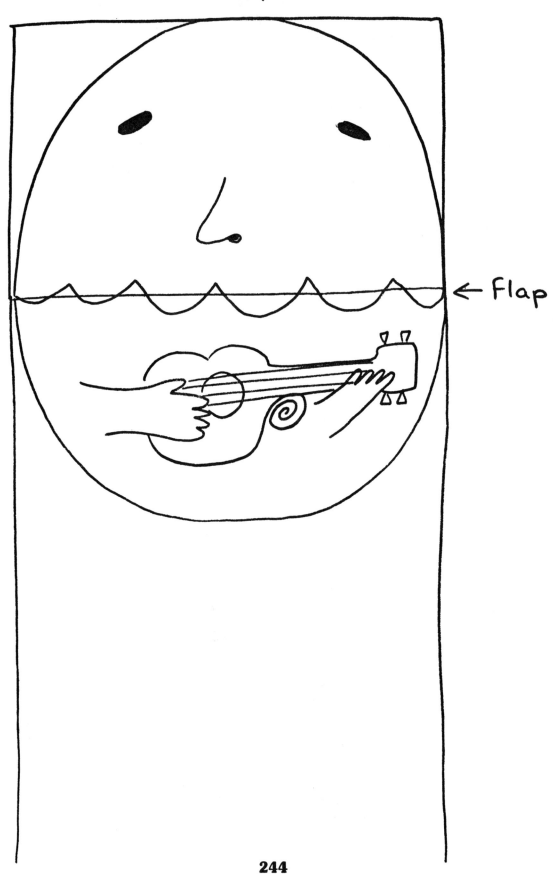

← Flap

We're Goin' Skatin'
dress-up figure

Who Is Friends with a Cat?

dress - up prop

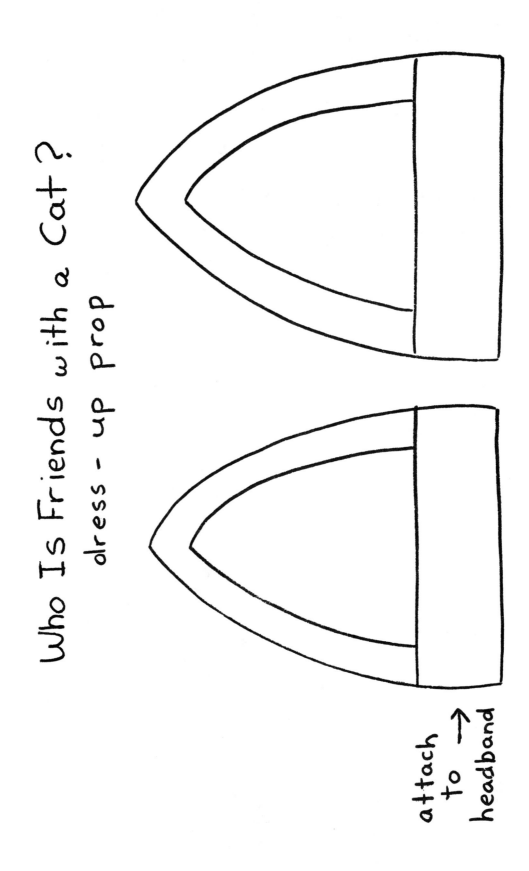

attach
to →
headband